THE German

HANDBOOK

Your guide to speaking and writing German

PAUL WEBSTER

REVISED EDITION

CAMBRIDGE
UNIVERSITY PRESS

Using the Handbook

If you are learning German – at school or as an adult learner – *The German Handbook* is for you. Here you can find out, from scratch, how the language works and how to use it accurately when you are speaking or writing everyday German. The essentials are – I hope – clearly explained, with small points and exceptions included where necessary and useful, but this is not an exhaustive grammar book. As well as grammar, the book contains a lot of material to help you express yourself both in speech and in writing (Chapters 12–15). This second edition includes some new material to make the Handbook more useful for those studying German to a higher level. It also incorporates the **Rechtschreibreform**. Nevertheless, the section numbering remains compatible with the first edition.

Paul Webster

Abbreviations used

acc.	accusative
adj.	adjective
dat.	dative
f.	feminine
gen.	genitive
inf.	infinitive
m.	masculine
neut.	neuter
nom.	nominative
pl.	plural
sing.	singular
usw.	**und so weiter** (= etc.)

Symbols used

*	verb which takes **sein** (see 10.22)
	points on which errors are very common
•	essential verbs on the verb list (see 10.43)

PUBLISHED BY THE PRESS SYNDICATE OF THE UNIVERSITY OF CAMBRIDGE
The Pitt Building, Trumpington Street, Cambridge, United Kingdom

CAMBRIDGE UNIVERSITY PRESS
The Edinburgh Building, Cambridge CB2 2RU, United Kingdom
40 West 20th Street, New York, NY 10011–4211, USA
10 Stamford Road, Oakleigh, VIC 3166, Australia
Ruiz de Alarcón 13, 28014 Madrid, Spain
Dock House, The Waterfront, Cape Town 8001, South Africa

http://www.cambridge.org

First published 1987
Second edition 1999
Reprinted 2000

Printed in the United Kingdom at the University Press, Cambridge

Typeset in Officina, Akzidence Grotesque and Rotis Semi-Sans

Designed by Angela Ashton   Illustrations by Ralf Zeigermann

A catalogue record for this book is available from the British Library

ISBN 0 521 64860 2 paperback

Contents

1 Nouns

1.1 What is a noun?

A noun is a word which names a thing, a person, a concept or anything else:

der Bus, die Freundschaft, das Land, der Mann, der Tag

Capital letters

German nouns must be written with a capital letter:

der **B**us, die **S**chule, das **K**lassenzimmer

1.2 The three genders

All German nouns belong to one of three large groups. These are known as the three genders – masculine, feminine and neuter. The markers and adjective forms used with each noun depend on which gender the noun belongs to; markers and adjectives are explained in Chapter 2. The words for people, things and concepts can belong to any of the three genders – there is not much logic about it. For example, the words for *knife*, *fork* and *spoon* each belong to a different gender:

spoon	**der** Löffel (m.)
fork	**die** Gabel (f.)
knife	**das** Messer (neut.)

The word for person is feminine (*die* **Person**), even when it refers to a man or boy, and the word for girl (*das* **Mädchen**) is neuter! The only way to cope with this is to regard the word for *the* (**der**, **die** or **das**) as part of each noun and learn it with the noun, so do not think of the word for *bus* as **Bus**, but as **der Bus**.

Although the genders are not logical, the following notes will help.

1.2a Masculine

Far more nouns are in the masculine than in either of the other genders. The following are masculine:

• days:	**der** Sonntag, **der** Mittwoch
• months:	**der** Mai, **der** Oktober
• seasons:	**der** Winter, **der** Herbst
• male persons:	**der** Mann, **der** Onkel, **der** Taxifahrer
• makes of car:	**der** Porsche, **der** VW-Golf (BUT: **das** Auto)
• many short nouns formed by removing **-en** from infinitives:	**der** Schlaf, **der** Anfang, **der** Schrei
• most nouns ending in **-el** or **-er**:	**der** Apfel, **der** Computer

1.2b Feminine

The following are feminine:

- female persons

  die Frau, **die** Schwester

  (UNLESS the noun ends in **-chen** or **-lein**: *das* Mädchen, *das* Fräulein)

- numbers

  Ich habe **eine** Eins geschrieben.
  I got a grade one.

- nouns with these endings:

-ei	**die** Bäckerei	*bakery*
-ie	**die** Drogerie	*chemists*
-ung	**die** Zeitung	*newspaper*
-heit	**die** Krankheit	*illness*
-keit	**die** Höflichkeit	*politeness*
-tion	**die** Information	*information*
-schaft	**die** Landschaft	*landscape*

- most words ending in **-e**:

  die Tomate, **die** Banane, **die** Rose

  (BUT: there are also some neuter nouns and some masculine nouns ending in **-e** such as **der Junge** (*boy*). See 1.6.)

1.2c Neuter

The following words are neuter:

- infinitives used as nouns:

  das Schwimmen   *swimming*

- words ending in **-chen** or **-lein**. These words usually refer to something small or young:

das Mädchen	*girl*
das Türchen	*little door*
das Kindlein	*little child*

- words ending in **-um** or **-ment** and most words ending in **-o**:

  das Museum, **das** Experiment, **das** Radio

 der See or **die See?**

der See	*lake*
die See	*sea* [= **das Meer**]

Both words have the plural **Seen** – pronounced **See-en**.

1.3 Compound nouns

German often puts two or more words together to make a new noun (known in grammar as a compound noun):

groß + **der** Vater ⤑ **der** Großvater *grandfather*

The gender of a compound noun is decided by the noun at the end of it:

das Auto + **die** Fabrik ⤑ **die** Autofabrik *car factory*

1.4 Plurals

German has a variety of ways of making nouns plural. When you learn a noun, it is useful to learn not only its gender but also its plural.

Dictionaries and vocabularies usually show how to form the plural in a shortened form, e.g. **das Buch** (¨er). This means that the plural is **Bücher**. Umlaut (¨) can be added to **a**, **o**, **u** and **au** (which becomes **äu**).

In a compound word, it is the last component which is affected, e.g. **der Großvater** (¨) has the plural **Großväter**. The following notes will give you some help with plurals.

1.4a Masculine plurals

A typical plural is **-e**, with Umlaut added if possible:

der Tisch (**-e**), der Schrank (**¨e**)

Here are some of the commonest exceptions:

der Tag (**-e**), der Hund (**-e**), der Arm (**-e**), der Schuh (**-e**), der Punkt (**-e**)

Masculine nouns ending in **-el**, **-en**, **-er** never add an ending in the plural, but some of them add Umlaut:

der Wagen (**–**), der Fahrer (**–**)
der Laden (**¨**), der Apfel (**¨**)

1.4b Feminine plurals

The most usual plural is **-n** or **-en**:

die Lampe (**-n**), die Frau (**-en**)

Words ending in **-in** add **-nen**:

die Freundin (**-nen**)

Most feminine nouns ending in **-el** or **-er** add **-n** for the plural:

die Tafel (**-n**), die Schwester (**-n**)

Exceptions: die Mutter (**¨**), die Tochter (**¨**)

Here are a few common feminine nouns which add **¨e**:

die Hand (**¨e**), die Wand (**¨e**), die Stadt (**¨e**), die Nacht (**¨e**), die Maus (**¨e**), die Kuh (**¨e**), usw.

1.4c Neuter plurals

Many common neuter nouns add **-e** (with no Umlaut):

> das Schaf (**-e**), das Haar (**-e**), das Spiel (**-e**), das Zelt (**-e**)

Many other neuter nouns add **-er**, with Umlaut if possible:

> das Kleid (**-er**), das Buch (**⁻er**)

Note these common neuter nouns, which unexpectedly have the plural **-n/-en**:

> das Auge (**-n**), das Ohr (**-en**), das Hemd (**-en**), das Bett (**-en**), das Ende (**-n**)

1.4d Plural in English, but singular in German

Here are some common examples:

die Brille	*pair of glasses*
die Hose	*pair of trousers*
die Schere	*pair of scissors*
die Treppe	*(flight of) stairs*

Diese Brille ist sehr schön.
These glasses are very nice.

1.4e Plural verb in English, but singular verb in German

There are some singular English nouns which we often use with a plural verb, such as family and police. These must have a singular verb in German.

> Die Familie Schmidt **macht** heute ein Picknick.
> The Schmidt family **are going** on a picnic today.

> Die Polizei **hat** den Dieb verhaftet.
> The police **have** arrested the thief.

1.4f Plural in German, but singular in English

die Möbel (pl.)	*(pieces of) furniture*
die Lebensmittel (pl.)	*food (i.e. groceries)*

Gute Lebensmittel **sind** teuer.
Good food **is** expensive.

1.5 Other noun endings

In the *genitive singular* of masculine and neuter nouns, **-s** or **-es** is added. Usually, **-es** is added to short words and **-s** to longer words, but this is not a strict rule (see 3.9).

> Das ist das Haus meines Freund(**e**)**s**.
> That is my friend's house.

This rule does not apply to weak nouns (see 1.6 below).

In the *dative plural*, **-n** is added to the noun plural, unless this already ends in **-n** or in **-s**:

> mit den Kinder**n**, mit den Frauen, mit den Baby**s**

1.6 Weak nouns

These nouns are a small group of masculine words which end in **-n** or **-en** in all their forms except for the nominative singular. An example is **der Junge** (*boy*).

	singular	plural
nom.	der Junge	die Jungen
acc.	den Jungen	die Jungen
gen.	des Jungen [no s]	der Jungen
dat.	dem Jungen	den Jungen

In vocabulary lists, this is shown as: **der Junge (-n, -n)** to make it clear that there is **-n** added in the singular as well as in the plural.

Here is a list of common weak nouns you will meet:

der Bauer (**-n**, **-n**)	*farmer*
der Franzose (**-n**, **-n**)	*Frenchman*
der Ire (**-n**, **-n**)	*Irishman*
der Journalist (**-en**,**-en**)	*journalist*
der Kunde (**-n**, **-n**)	*customer*
der Matrose (**-n**, **-n**)	*sailor*
der Mensch (**-en**, **-en**)	*person, human being*
der Nachbar (**-n**, **-n**)	*neighbour*
der Name (**-n**, **-n**)*	*name*
der Neffe (**-n**, **-n**)	*nephew*
der Pilot (**-en**, **-en**)	*pilot*
der Polizist (**-en**, **-en**)	*policeman*
der Russe (**-en**, **-en**)	*Russian*
der Schotte (**-n**, **-n**)	*Scot*
der Soldat (**-en**, **-en**)	*soldier*
der Student (**-en**, **-en**)	*student*
der Tourist (**-en**, **-en**)	*tourist*

*This word has an irregular genitive: **des Namens**.

Herr (meaning **Mr** or **gentleman**) adds **-n** in the singular but **-en** in the plural.

Herr Müller ist krank. (nom.)
Herr Müller is ill.

Hast du Herr**n** Schmidt gesehen? (acc.)
Have you seen Herr Schmidt?

Das ist Herr**n** Brauns Auto. (gen.)
That's Herr Braun's car.

Kann ich mit Herr**n** Grün sprechen ? (dat.)
Can I speak to Herr Grün?

Die beiden Herr**en** sind da. (nom. pl.)
The two gentlemen are here.

1.7 Adjectival nouns

These are nouns which have endings as if they were adjectives – the word **Mann** or **Frau** is understood:

der deutsch**e** Mann	·····⟩	der Deutsch**e**
ein deutsch**er** Mann	·····⟩	ein Deutsch**er**
eine deutsch**e** Frau	·····⟩	eine Deutsch**e**

(For the details of the possible adjective endings, see Chapter 2.)

NOTE that these nouns begin with a capital letter, like other nouns. Other adjectival nouns you are likely to meet are:

der Verwandte	*relative*
der Bekannte	*acquaintance, friend*
der Beamte	*official, civil servant*

For the endings to use after the personal pronouns **wir** and **ihr**, see 2.8.

beide and *andere*

These have similar endings but they do not have capital letters. These examples show them in use:

Jens und Renate gehen **beide** ins Kino.
Jens and Renate are **both** going to the cinema.

Die beiden gehen ins Kino.
The two of them are going to the cinema.

Jutta blieb zu Hause. **Die anderen** gingen in die Disko.
Jutta stayed at home. **The others** went to the disco.

2 Markers, adjectives and adverbs

2.1 What is a marker?

Nouns do not usually stand alone; they are normally 'introduced' by words such as **der**, **ein**, **mein**, **dieser**. In this book such words are called 'markers' – you can think of them as 'marking out' the nouns. There is a fixed number of them, and they are all given in this chapter together with their own special endings systems. They often introduce adjectives as well. This table shows all three in action:

marker	adjective	noun
der	neue	Supermarkt
eine	alte	Dame
diese	furchtbare	Grammatik
mein		Opa
	gute	Freunde

NOTE that there need not always be both a marker and an adjective.

2.2 What is an adjective?

Adjectives are words that describe.

> Jan ist **intelligent.**
> Jan ist ein **intelligenter** Junge.

In the first example, the adjective **intelligent** stands alone (not directly in front of the noun it describes). In German, adjectives which stand alone have no endings. In the second example, the adjective directly describes the noun **Junge**. When an adjective is in this position in German, it must have an adjective ending.

2.3 The three systems for markers and adjectives

German has three systems of ending for markers and adjectives. This means three tables to learn! It is not quite as complicated as it seems at first, because many of the endings are the same in the different tables. These examples show the three types:

2.3a *der/die/das* system

> **Das Postamt** ist nicht weit von hier.
> **Das neue Postamt** ist nicht weit von hier.
> **Dieser Pullover** ist sehr warm.

For details, see 2.4 and 2.5.

2.3b   *ein/eine/ein* system

> **Eine Jeansjacke** ist nicht so teuer wie **eine Lederjacke.**
> **Eine gute Lederjacke** ist natürlich teuer.
> **Meine Katze** heißt Mitzi.
> **Unser neues Haus** hat drei Schlafzimmer.

For details, see 2.6 and 2.7.

2.3c   'No marker' system

> **Viele Schüler** lernen Deutsch.
> **Viele englische Schüler** lernen Deutsch.

For details, see 2.8.

2.4   The *der/die/das* system

These tables show the endings used on markers (and adjectives if used) for the **der/die/das** system. The tables show the four cases (for explanation of cases, see Chapter 3) and the three genders, in both singular and plural.

Singular

	m.	**f.**	**neut.**
nom.	**der** gute Mann	**die** gute Frau	**das** gute Kind
acc.	**den** guten Mann	**die** gute Frau	**das** gute Kind
gen.	**des** guten Mannes	**der** guten Frau	**des** guten Kindes
dat.	**dem** guten Mann	**der** guten Frau	**dem** guten Kind

Plural

In the plural, the three genders have identical endings:

nom.	**die** guten Männer/Frauen/Kinder
acc.	**die** guten Männer/Frauen/Kinder
gen.	**der** guten Männer/Frauen/Kinder
dat.	**den** guten Männern/Frauen/Kindern

NOTE that there are several marker forms (e.g. **der**, **die**, **das**, **den**), but only two adjective endings: **-e** and **-en**. The toothbrush-shaped shading in the singular table divides these: **-e** within the shading and **-en** below it, including all of the plural.

2.5   The other markers of the *der/die/das* type

There are a few other markers which follow the same pattern as **der/die/das** and which are followed by the same system of adjective endings. The most common is **dieser** (*this*):

Singular

	m.	f.	neut.
nom.	dies**er**	dies**e**	dies**es**
acc.	dies**en**	dies**e**	dies**es**
gen.	dies**es**	dies**er**	dies**es**
dat.	dies**em**	dies**er**	dies**em**

Plural

nom.	dies**e**
acc.	dies**e**
gen.	dies**er**
dat.	dies**en**

NOTE that the endings for **dieser** closely resemble **der/die/das**. The only difference is that the neuter nominative and accusative have **-es** (dies**es**), where the **der/die/das** table has **das**.

Other markers of this type are:

jeder/jede/jedes	*each, every*
welcher?/welche?/welches?	*which?*
mancher/manche/manches	*many a, some*
jener/jene/jenes*	*that*

*Not very common, because **der/die/das** are mostly used for the meaning *that*.

2.6 The *ein/eine/ein* system

This table shows the endings used on markers (and adjectives if used) for the **ein/eine/ein** system. The tables shows the four cases (for explanation of cases, see Chapter 3) and the three genders, in both singular and plural.

Singular

	m.	f.	neut.
nom.	ein guter Mann	eine gute Frau	ein gutes Kind
acc.	einen guten Mann	eine gute Frau	ein gutes Kind
gen.	eines guten Mannes	einer guten Frau	eines guten Kindes
dat.	einem guten Mann	einer guten Frau	einem guten Kind

Plural

In the plural, the three genders have identical endings. **ein** does not have a plural (just as in English we cannot say 'a men' or 'a women'), so the table uses another marker of the same type – **kein**:

nom.	**keine** guten Männer/Frauen/Kinder
acc.	**keine** guten Männer/Frauen/Kinder
gen.	**keiner** guten Männer/Frauen/Kinder
dat.	**keinen** guten Männer**n**/Frauen/Kinder**n**

NOTE that this system is different from the **der/die/das** system only within the toothbrush-shaped shading. Below the shading, both marker and adjective have the same endings as on the **der/die/das** table. It is only within the shading that the two marker systems differ.

2.7   The other markers of the *ein/eine/ein* type

Several other markers follow exactly the same pattern as **ein/eine/ein**. These are the possessives and **kein**:

mein	*my*	
dein	*your*	(corresponds to **du**, see 4.3)
sein	*his, its*	
ihr	*her, its*	
sein	*its*	
unser	*our*	
euer	*your*	(corresponds to **ihr**, see 4.3)
Ihr	*your*	(corresponds to **Sie**, see 4.3)
ihr	*their*	
kein	*not a, no*	

Meine neue Hose ist blau.
My new trousers are blue.

Das ist **unser neues Auto**.
That's **our new car**.

Karin geht mit **ihrem Freund** aus.
Karin is going out with **her boyfriend**.

NOTE that **kein** must be used instead of 'nicht ein'. (See also 9.12.)

Das ist **kein** Kuli [NOT ~~nicht ein Kuli~~], das ist ein Füller.
That is**n't a** ball-point, it's a fountain pen.

2.8   The 'no marker' system

Sometimes, nouns and adjectives are used without any marker. In most cases, German then gives the adjective or adjectives the endings that a marker would have had, if it had been used.

Viel**e** jung**e** Engländer lernen Deutsch.

NOTE that **viele** is not a marker. In this example we simply have two adjectives (**viele** and **junge**) with a noun (**Engländer**). The 'no marker' system is mainly needed in the plural, less often in the singular.

Singular

	m.	f.	neut.
nom.	gut**er** Wein	gut**e** Suppe	gut**es** Bier
acc.	gut**en** Wein	gut**e** Suppe	gut**es** Bier
gen.	gut**en** Wein(e)s	gut**er** Suppe	gut**en** Bier(e)s
dat.	gut**em** Wein	gut**er** Suppe	gut**em** Bier

NOTE the unexpected genitive forms for masculine and neuter.

<u>Plural</u>

nom.	**viele gute** Bücher
acc.	**viele gute** Bücher
gen.	**vieler guter** Bücher
dat.	**vielen guten** Büchern

Apart from **viele**, other adjectives often used in this way are **einige** (*some*), and **wenige** (*few*). The 'no marker' endings are also needed after *numbers* (**zwei** neue Bücher, etc.), **mehr** (*more*) and **weniger** (*fewer*).

<u>Endings after personal pronouns</u>

After personal prononouns such as **ich** and **du**, the 'no marker' endings are needed (e.g. **du arm*er* Junge**), but after **wir** and **ihr**, **-en** is used in the nominative plural, where you would expect to find **-e**.

nom.	wir jung**en** Leute	ihr jung**en** Leute
acc.	uns jung**e** Leute	euch jung**e** Leute
dat.	uns jung**en** Leuten	euch jung**en** Leuten

EXCEPTIONS: **wir beide** and **wir Deutsche** are more common than the alternatives with **-en.**

2.9 Adjectives – endings difficulties in the plural: *-e* or *-en?*

If there is *any marker* (see 2.5 and 2.7), the adjective ending is **-en** in the nominative and accusative plural:

die
meine
unsere } neu**en** Freunde
diese
keine

NOTE that **alle**, and (usually) **beide** and **solche**, are used like this too:

alle
beide } neu**en** Freunde
solche

When there is *no marker,* the adjective ending is **-e** in the nominative and accusative plural. Here are just a few of the possibilities:

viele
manche*
einige } neu**e** Freunde
wenige
mehr
zwei

*manche** can also follow the other pattern: **manche neu*en* Freunde.**

For the adjective endings to use after **wir** and **ihr**, see 2.8.

2.10 How to express *some* and *any*

 In German there is usually no need for the equivalent of the English words *some* and *any*.

> Haben Sie Brot da?
> Have you **any** bread?

> Ich will Wurst kaufen.
> I want to buy **some** sausage.

> Ich habe Eier gekauft.
> I bought **some** eggs.

In negative sentences, **kein** is often required:

> Ich habe **keine** Geschwister.
> I have**n't** got **any** brothers or sisters.

etwas is used in the singular to mean *a bit of*, and **einige** is used in the plural to mean *a few* (see also 4.12).

> Er hat **etwas** Suppe gegessen.
> He ate **some** [= a bit of] soup.

> Er hat **einige** Kekse gegessen.
> He ate **some** [= a few] biscuits.

When the meaning of *any* is *every possible* or *all possible*, **jeder/jede/jedes** (see 2.5) is needed in the singuar and **alle** in the plural:

> **Jedes Kind** kann dir sagen, dass Zigaretten ungesund sind.
> **Any child** can tell you that cigarettes are unhealthy.

> Ich bin gegen **alle neuen Straßen** in Deutschland.
> I am against **any new roads** in Germany.

irgendein (and other words starting with **irgend-**) only correspond to *some* and *any* in the meaning *some ... or other* or *any ... at all*:

> Er ist mit **irgendeinem Schulkameraden** unterwegs.
> He's out with **some schoolmate or other**.

> Hast du **irgendeine Idee**, wie wir dieses Problem lösen können?
> Have you **any idea** (**at all**) how we can solve this problem?

In the plural, this becomes **irgendwelche**:

> Hat es **irgendwelche Anrufe** gegeben?
> Have there been **any phone calls** (**at all**)?

NOTE also:

irgendwo	*somewhere, anywhere*
jemand (ALSO: irgendjemand)	*someone, somebody, anyone, anybody*
etwas (ALSO: irgendetwas)	*something* (in conversation often shortened to **was** and **irgendwas**)
irgendwie	*somehow*
irgendwann	*sometime*
manchmal	*sometimes*

2.11 *the same: derselbe and der gleiche*

derselbe means *the one and the same* person or thing:

Jochen und Hans gehen in **dieselbe** Schule.
Jochen and Hans go to **the same** school.

der gleiche means an *identically similar* person or thing:

Jochen und Hans tragen **den gleichen** Pullover.
Jochen and Hans are wearing **the same** pullover. [i.e. two identical ones!]

With both expressions, normal marker and adjective endings are needed.

> **der gleiche** is written as two words; **derselbe** is written as one word. BUT NOTE these alternatives – both are correct:
>
> Petra und Helga arbeiten **in demselben / im selben** Kaufhaus.
> Petra and Helga work **in the same** department store.
>
> When the **der/die/das** part of **derselbe** is combined with a preposition (here: **im**), the preposition is written separately.

2.12 Invariables

Unlike most other adjectives, the following words are *invariable* – which means they never vary their endings. These are the commonest ones:

mehr	*more*
weniger	*less, fewer*
genug	*enough*
ein paar	*a few*

Dieter hat **mehr** Geld als ich.
Dieter has **more** money than I have.

Ich habe **weniger** Geld als er.
I have **less** money than he has.

Bekommst du **genug** Taschengeld?
Do you get **enough** pocket-money?

Ich gehe mit **ein paar** Freunden aus.
I'm going out with **a few** friends.

viel (*much, a lot of, many*) and **wenig** (*little, not much*) usually have no endings in the singular*, but normal endings in the plural:

Die Engländer trinken **viel** Tee.
The English drink **a lot of** tea.

Sie essen **viele** Pommes frites.
They eat **a lot of** chips.

Ich habe **wenig** Freizeit.
I have **little / not much** free time.

Er hat **wenige** Freunde.
He has **few** friends.

> *BUT NOTE: viel**en** Dank (*many thanks*).

2.13   Adjectives formed from the names of towns and cities

These adjectives end in **-er** – an ending which never varies in any way:

> Die **Londoner** Busse sind rot.
> The **London** buses are red.

> die **Hamburger** U-Bahn
> the **Hamburg** underground

One adjective from a country is made in this way – **Schweizer** (*Swiss*):

> Ich habe eine **Schweizer** Uhr gekauft.
> I have bought a **Swiss** watch.

2.14   Adjectives and adverbs

<u>What is an adverb?</u>

Just as adjectives give more information about nouns, so adverbs do the same for verbs. In German a large group of words play a double role – they are both adjectives *and* adverbs.

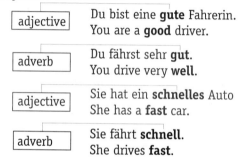

adjective	Du bist eine **gute** Fahrerin. You are a **good** driver.
adverb	Du fährst sehr **gut**. You drive very **well**.
adjective	Sie hat ein **schnelles** Auto She has a **fast** car.
adverb	Sie fährt **schnell**. She drives **fast**.

NOTE that when used as an adverb, the word has no ending.

Remember that an adjective also has no ending when it stands alone (see 2.2):

> Jan ist **intelligent**.   adjective

2.15   How to compare

2.15a   The comparative

In English we compare by adding *-er* to adjectives, or by using the word *more*:

> Peter is **younger** than John, but John is **more childish**.

German uses only the first method:

> Brigitte ist **intelligenter als** Ulrike.
> Brigitte is **more intelligent than** Ulrike.

NOTE that **als** is used for *than*.

Some common short adjectives (and adverbs such as **oft**) add Umlaut as well as **-er**. These are the ones you are likely to need:

alt/älter	*old/older (elder)*
arm/ärmer	*poor/poorer*
dumm/dümmer	*stupid / more stupid*
gesund/gesünder	*healthy/healthier*
groß/größer	*big/bigger, tall/taller*
hart/härter	*hard/harder*
jung/jünger	*young/younger*
kalt/kälter	*cold/colder*
klug/klüger	*clever/cleverer*
kurz/kürzer	*short/shorter*
lang/länger	*long/longer*
nah/näher	*near/nearer*
oft/öfter	*often / more often*
scharf/schärfer	*sharp/sharper*
schmal/schmäler	*narrow/narrower*
schwach/schwächer	*weak/weaker*
stark/stärker	*strong/stronger*
warm/wärmer	*warm/warmer*

Here are some short adjectives which do *not* add Umlaut (although you might expect them to):

faul/fauler	*lazy/lazier*
flach/flacher	*flat/flatter*
froh/froher	*happy/happier*
klar/klarer	*clear/clearer*
rund/runder	*round/rounder*
schlank/schlanker	*slim/slimmer*
voll/voller	*full/fuller*

These comparatives of adjectives and adverbs are irregular:

gut/besser	*good/better*
viel/mehr	*much/more*
hoch/höher	*high/higher*
gern/lieber	*gladly / by preference**

*Used to express liking – see 12.4g–i.

Comparatives are used in the same way as other adjectives. This means that they need adjective endings when they come before a noun:

Dieser Pullover ist **billiger** als der. [no ending needed]
This pullover is **cheaper** than that one.

Ich kaufe den **billigeren** Pullover. [normal adjective ending]
I'll buy the **cheaper** pullover.

NOTE the word order normally used in sentences like this:

Frauen können Hausarbeit besser machen als Männer.
Peter kann nicht so schnell laufen wie sein Bruder.

The **als** and **wie** phrases are held back until the end of the sentence.

2.15b   Other methods of comparison – using *wie*

Margarine schmeckt nicht **so** gut **wie** Butter.
Margarine does not taste **as** good **as** butter.

Du schwimmst **genauso** gut **wie** ich.
You swim just **as** well **as** I do.

Peter hat **fast soviel** Geld **wie** Uwe.
Peter has **almost as much** money **as** Uwe.

2.16   The superlative

In English we add *-est* to adjectives, or we use the word *most*:

Karen gets the **biggest** salary, yet Anne is the **most conscientious** employee.

German uses only the first method, but usually adds **-st-** not **-est-** to the adjective:

Udo ist der **faulste** Schüler der Klasse. [NOTE normal adjective ending]
Udo is the **laziest** pupil in the class.

The adjectives which add Umlaut in the comparative also add Umlaut in the superlative (see the list in 2.15):

Susanne ist das **jüngste** Mädchen der Klasse.
Susanne is the **youngest** girl in the class.

To make the pronunciation of superlatives easier, **-est-** is added to some adjectives. Typically, this happens with those ending in **-t, -d, -s, -ß, -z, -sch**:

der intelligent**e**ste Junge
the most intelligent boy

der süß**e**ste Wein
the sweetest wine

Often the superlative does not precede a noun, but comes elsewhere in the sentence. Then the usual form is **am ...-sten**:

Äpfel sind teuer, Birnen sind teurer, aber Melonen sind **am teuersten**.
Apples are dear, pears are dearer but melons are **the dearest**.

Jan läuft schnell, Uwe läuft schneller, aber Falk läuft **am schnellsten**.
Jan runs fast, Uwe runs faster, but Falk runs **the fastest**.

Irregular superlatives

gut ⟶ **besser** ⟶ **der beste / am besten**
good ⟶ better ⟶ the best / best

viel ⟶ **mehr** ⟶ **der meiste / am meisten**
much ⟶ more ⟶ the most / most

hoch ⟶ **höher** ⟶ **der höchste / am höchsten**
high ⟶ higher ⟶ the highest / highest

groß ---> **größer** ---> **der größte / am größten**
big   ---> bigger ---> the biggest / biggest OR
tall ---> taller ---> the tallest / tallest

nah ---> **näher** ---> **der nächste / am nächsten**
near ---> nearer ---> the nearest OR the next

gern ---> **lieber** ---> **am liebsten**
(used to express liking – see 12.4g–12.4i)

2.17 Special uses of *der/die/das*

The marker **der/die/das** is used in some situations where we would not use *the* in English:

a The marker is normally used with nouns which have an abstract or generalised sense:

Der deutsche Alltag
German daily life

Die Umweltverschmutzung ist ein großes Problem.
Pollution is a big problem.

b With parts of the body or clothing, when the owner is obvious:

Ich habe mir **die** Hände gewaschen.
I washed **my** hands.

(See also 10.7b.)

c With days, months, seasons, meals and streets:

am [= an **dem**] Mittwoch	*on Wednesday*
im [= in **dem**] Januar	*in January*
im [= in **dem**] Sommer	*in Summer*
nach **dem** Frühstück	*after breakfast*
er wohnt in **der** Goethestraße	*he lives in Goethestrasse*

d To express price per quantity:

Die Tomaten kosten einen Euro **das** Kilo.
The tomatoes cost one Euro **a** kilo.

(See also 6.6c.)

e With the names of a few countries, a common example of which is **die Schweiz** (*Switzerland*):

Ich fahre **in die** Schweiz. [NOT ~~nach~~]
I'm going **to** Switzerland.

Urs kommt **aus der** Schweiz.
Urs comes **from** Switzerland.

Er wohnt **in der** Schweiz.
He lives **in** Switzerland.

Other similar ones are:

die Bundesrepublik Deutschland	*the Federal Republic of Germany*
die Sowjetunion	*the Soviet Union*

die Türkei	*Turkey*
die Niederlande (pl.)	*the Netherlands*
die USA (pl.)	*the USA*

 NOTE: with most countries, however, **der/die/das** is not needed (i.e. as in English):

Ich fahre **nach Deutschland**.
I'm going **to Germany**.

Ich komme **aus England**.
I come **from England**.

Ich wohne **in Schottland**.
I live **in Scotland**.

f   In some set phrases:

Ich gehe in **die** Schule.	*I go to school.*
Wir sind in **der** Schule.	*We are at school.*
Ich gehe in **die** Stadt.	*I'm going to town / into town.*
Wir waren in **der** Stadt.	*We were in town.*
Ich gehe **ins** Bett.	*I'm going to bed.*
Bleiben Sie **im** Bett!	*Stay in bed!*
Ich gehe in **die** Kirche.	*I'm going to church.*
Ich fahre mit **dem** Bus, usw.	*I'm going by bus, etc.*

2.18   Omission of *ein*

a   After the verbs **sein** and **werden** to show jobs, positions in life or nationalities, the marker **ein/eine/ein** is not required:

Meine Mutter ist Ärztin.
My mother is **a** doctor.

Mein Bruder ist Student.
My brother is **a** student.

Ich will Architektin werden.
I want to become **an** architect.

Ich bin Engländer/Engländerin.
I'm **an** Englishman/Englishwoman.

However, the marker is used when an adjective is included:

Ihr Vater ist **ein berühmter Maler**.
Her father is **a famous painter**.

b   Often after **mit** and **ohne** and in some set phrases:

ein Zimmer mit Dusche
a room with **a** shower

Ohne Schläger kann ich nicht spielen.
I can't play without **a** racket.

Ich habe Husten.
I've got **a** cough.

3 Cases and prepositions

3.1 What are cases?

Look at these four English examples:

1 **My uncle** visits us often.
2 We often telephone **my uncle**.
3 At Christmas I gave **my uncle** a present.
4 We spent the holiday with **my uncle**.

The words *my uncle* stay exactly the same in all four sentences, even though grammatically *my uncle* has a different role in each sentence.

1 In the first sentence, *my uncle* is the *subject* – the person or thing that 'does' the action expressed by the verb (here, it is the uncle who 'does' the visiting).

2 In the second sentence, *my uncle* is the *direct object* – the person or thing on the receiving end of the action (the verb *telephone*); here it is the uncle who 'gets' telephoned.

3 In the third sentence, *my uncle* is the indirect object. The verb used here (*gave* from the verb *give*) can have two objects. The thing actually given (*a present*) is the direct object, and *my uncle* is the indirect object – the person or thing that the action is done *for* or *to*. Another way of saying this sentence would be: At Christmas I gave a present *to* my uncle.

4 In the fourth sentence, *my uncle* has yet another role – in a phrase introduced by a *preposition* (here it is the preposition *with*).

In English, we mostly rely on the order of words to make clear what is the subject, what is the direct object, etc. German does more than this, however:

> Der Hund biss den Briefträger.
> The dog bit the postman.

Here, *the dog* is the subject (it 'does' the biting) and *the postman* is the direct object (he 'gets' bitten). If we alter the order of words in the English version, we completely alter the meaning!

> The postman bit the dog.

But the German sentence can be rearranged without affecting the meaning:

> Den Briefträger biss der Hund.

This still means *The dog bit the postman*. German is here not relying on the order of words. It uses its cases to show the subject and direct object. The markers (for details see Chapter 2) **den** and **der** show the roles played by the postman and the dog.

There are four cases: nominative, accusative, genitive and dative. Their various uses are dealt with in the following sections. (For details of the marker and adjective endings associated with the cases, see 2.4–2.9. For details of pronouns in the various cases, see 4.1–4.5.)

3.2   Nominative

a   The nominative is the form found in dictionaries and vocabulary lists:

der Mann, die Frau, das Kind

b   It must be used to show the *subject* of a sentence. The subject is the person or thing that 'does' the action expressed by the verb:

Mein kleiner Bruder kaufte einen neuen Kassettenrecorder.
My little brother bought a new cassette recorder.

 It need not come before the verb:

Gestern kaufte **mein kleiner Bruder** einen neuen Kassettenrecorder.
Yesterday **my little brother** bought a new cassette recorder.

c   The nominative is used after the verb **sein** (*to be*) and with **werden** (*to become*):

Herr Meyer ist **ein alter Lehrer.**
Herr Meyer is **an old teacher.**

Mein Bruder will **Beamter** werden.
My brother wants to become **a civil servant.**

 Avoid the common mistake of using accusative after these two verbs!

3.3   Accusative

a   The main use of the accusative is to show the *direct object* of a sentence. The direct object is the person or thing that is on the 'receiving end' of the verb:

Petra hat **einen Rucksack** gekauft.
Petra has bought **a rucksack.**

The rucksack is the direct object here because it is the thing that 'gets' bought.

 Direct objects are not always as easy to spot as in the example given above – it is not always the item following the verb! Here are some examples of slightly less obvious direct objects:

Gestern Abend hat ein Einbrecher **unseren Fernseher** gestohlen.
Yesterday evening, a burglar stole **our television set.**

Wen hast du besucht?
Whom did you visit?

Welchen Dom hast du besichtigt? [see also 2.5]
Which cathedral did you look round?

Der Pullover, **den** ich gekauft habe, ist grau. [see also 9.9]
The pullover (**that**) I have bought is grey.

b The accusative is also used after some prepositions – see 3.4 and 3.7.

c The accusative is used in some time expressions – see 7.6.

d The accusative is used in some expressions of measurement – see 6.7.

3.4 Prepositions with the accusative

<u>What are prepositions?</u>

Prepositions are words used before nouns and pronouns to show various kinds of connections and relationships between the items in sentences. Some English examples are: *with, for, under, between, before, after, in.*

These five German prepositions 'trigger off' the accusative in the words that follow them:

durch	*through*
für	*for*
gegen	*against*
ohne	*without*
um	*(a)round*

Wir wanderten **durch den Wald.**
We hiked **through the wood.**

Das ist ein Geschenk **für dich.**
This is a present **for you.**

Ich spielte **gegen meinen Bruder.**
I played **against my brother.**

Geht **ohne mich** ins Kino!
Go to the cinema **without me.**

Meine Freundin wohnt **um die Ecke.**
My friend lives **round the corner.**

> NOTE that **entlang** (*along*) also takes the accusative, but it follows the word it refers to:
>
> Gehen Sie **diese Straße entlang.**
> Go **along this street.**

3.5 Dative

a The main use of the dative is to show the *indirect* object of a sentence.

Some verbs can have two objects – one direct object (see 3.1 and 3.3) and one indirect object. With these verbs, the indirect object is the person or thing that the action is done *for* or *to*. Here are some English examples with the verbs and indirect objects emphasised in bold type:

I **gave my sister** a calculator.
I **wrote my penfriend** a long letter.
I **showed my parents** the photos I had taken.

Here are the same examples in German. The indirect objects are in the dative (in bold type):

Ich schenkte **meiner Schwester** einen Taschenrechner.
Ich schrieb **meinem Brieffreund** einen langen Brief.
Ich zeigte **meinen Eltern** die Fotos, die ich gemacht hatte.

Dative forms normally involve the endings:

-em	or	**-m**	(m. and neut. sing.)
-er	or	**-r**	(f. sing.)
-en	or	**-n**	(pl.)

(See the tables of endings in 2.4–2.6.)

In the dative plural, nouns add **-n** to their plural form, unless this already ends in **-n** or in **-s** (see 1.5).

 Indirect objects are not always easy to spot. Here are some examples of less obvious indirect objects:

Wem hast du das Buch gegeben?
To whom have you given the book? [in conversation: **Who** have you given the book **to**?]

Die Brieffreundin, **der** ich die Karte geschickt habe, wohnt in Wien.
The penfriend I sent the card **to** [**to whom** I sent the card] lives in Vienna.

b   The dative is also used after some prepositions – see 3.6 and 3.7.

c   Some verbs are followed by the dative (although you would expect a direct object in the accusative!) – see 10.30.

3.6   Prepositions with the dative

What are prepositions? (see 3.4)

These nine prepositions always 'trigger off' the dative in the words which follow them:

aus	*out of, from*
außer	*apart from, except*
bei	*with, at, at the house of, near*
gegenüber	*opposite*
mit	*with*
nach	*after; to* (with place names – see 3.8)
seit	*since, for* (see 7.3)
von	*of, from*
zu	*to* (see 3.8)

Um acht gehe ich **aus dem Haus**.
At eight I go **out of the house**.

Außer dir fahren alle mit.
Apart from you, everybody's going.

Ich wohnte **bei meinem Onkel**.
I stayed/lived **with my uncle**. [= at my uncle's house]

Wir wohnen **gegenüber der Bank.**
We live **opposite the bank.**

Ich fahre **mit meinen Eltern** hin.
I'm going there **with my parents.**

Nach dem Frühstück gehe ich zur Schule.
After breakfast I go to school.

Ich lerne **seit drei Jahren** Deutsch.
I've been learning German **for three years.**

Das ist ein Brief **von der Bank.**
This is a letter **from the bank.**

Das ist das Auto **von meiner Mutter.**
This is **my mother's** car.

Ich gehe **zum [= zu dem] Bahnhof.**
I'm going **to the station.**

Short forms

These are not compulsory, but they are usual:

bei + dem	·····⟩	**beim**
von + dem	·····⟩	**vom**
zu + dem	·····⟩	**zum**
zu + der	·····⟩	**zur**

Notes

1 **gegenüber** often follows the word it refers to:

Wir wohnen der Bank **gegenüber.**

2 **zu** means *at* not *to* in the phrase **zu Hause** (*at home*).

3 The short form **beim** is used before an infinitive in expressions such as:

beim Essen   *while eating*
beim Tanzen   *while dancing*

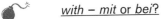

with – mit or bei?

mit is the most general word for *with*:

Ralf ging **mit Petra** ins Kino.
Ralf went to the cinema **with Petra.**

Ich esse Steak **mit Salat.**
I'm having steak **with salad.**

bei must be used when the meaning is *near, at the same place as* or *at the house of*:

Ich wohnte **bei meiner Tante.**
I stayed/lived **with my aunt.** [= at my aunt's house].

Ich stand **bei meinem Koffer.**
I stood **near/by my suitcase.**

NOTE that **bei** should not be used to mean *to the house of*. The word to use here is **zu**:

Ich fahre **zu meiner Tante.**
I'm going **to my aunt's.**

NOTE also that **bei** is used in some job situations:

Ich arbeite **bei der Post.**
I work **for the post office.**

Sie arbeitet **bei einer Bank.**
She works **for a bank.**

3.7   Motion and positions: prepositions with accusative and dative

German makes a clear distinction between *motion from place to place* and *position*.

NOTE that motion within one place counts as position:

Wir schwammen **im Fluß.**
We swam **in the river.**

Here are the nine prepositions which take *accusative to show motion* and *dative to show position*:

an		*at, on, up to*
auf		*on, on top of*
hinter		*behind*
in		*in, into, to* (compare 3.8)
neben		*next to, beside*
über		*over, above, across*
unter		*under, among*
vor		*in front of, outside, before*
zwischen		*between*

Examples

Accusative – motion

Gehen Sie **an die Kasse!**
Go **to the cash-desk.**

Stell das **auf den Tisch!**
Put that **on the table!**

Der Lehrer ging **hinter den Tisch.**
The teacher went **behind the desk.**

Ich gehe **in die Küche**
I'm going **into the kitchen.**

Dative – position

Man zahlt **an der Kasse.**
You pay **at the cash-desk.**

Das Brot ist **auf dem Tisch.**
The bread is **on the table.**

Der Lehrer stand **hinter dem Tisch.**
The teacher stood **behind the desk.**

Ich koche **in der Küche.**
I'm cooking **in the kitchen.**

über

NOTE that as well as meaning *over, above* and *across*, **über** is also used to mean *about*. When it means *about*, it always takes the accusative:

Wir gingen **über die Brücke.**
We went **over/across the bridge.**

Wir gingen **über die Straße.**
We went **across the road.** / We crossed the road.

Das ist ein Buch **über die Deutschen.**
This is a book **about the Germans.**

Short forms

These are the common ones. They are not compulsory, but they are usual:

an + das	⟶	**ans**
an + dem	⟶	**am**
auf + das	⟶	**aufs**
in + das	⟶	**ins**
in + dem	⟶	**im**

Useful expressions of motion and position

In many other expressions, German distinguishes motion and position. Here are a few examples:

Motion

Komm **hierher!**/Komm **her!***
Come **here!**

Wir gingen gestern **dorthin/dahin/hin.***
We went **there** yesterday.

Ich gehe **nach Hause.**
I'm going **home.**

Wir fahren **aufs** [= **auf das**] **Land.**
We're going **to the country(side).**

Ich fahre **ins Ausland.**
I'm going **abroad.**

Ich gehe **nach oben.**
I'm going **upstairs.**

Ich gehe **nach unten.**
I'm going **downstairs.**

Position

Wir wohnen **hier.**
We live **here.**

Wir waren gestern **dort/da.**
We were **there** yesterday.

Um fünf komme ich **zu Hause** an.
At five o'clock I arrive (at) **home.**

Wir wohnen **auf dem Land/Lande.**
We live **in the country(side).**

Ich möchte gern **im Ausland** wohnen.
I'd like to live **abroad.**

Mein Zimmer ist **oben.**
My room is **upstairs.**

Das Wohnzimmer ist **unten.**
The living-room is **downstairs.**

*For details of **hin** and **her**, see 10.6a.

3.8   How to express *to*

 a   **nach** is used with place names:

> Ich fahre **nach Wien**.
> I'm going **to Vienna**.
>
> Ich fahre **nach Italien**.
> I'm going **to Italy**.

> EXCEPTION: countries which have **die/der** before them (see 2.17e).
> Ich fahre **in die** Schweiz.
> I'm going **to** Switzerland.
>
> Ich fahre **in die** USA.
> I'm going **to the** United States.

b   **zu** + *dative* is used in most other instances:

> Ich gehe **zur Post**.
> I'm going to the **post office**.
>
> Ich gehe **zum Bahnhof**.
> I'm going **to the station**.

c   **in** + *accusative* is used to express going to a place, then going inside the place for a while:

> Ich gehe **ins Kino**.
> I'm going **to the cinema**.
>
> Ich gehe **ins Restaurant**.
> I'm going **to the restaurant**. / I'm going out for a meal.

> If **zum** were used instead of **ins** in these examples, it would give the impression of going to the cinema – but without seeing a film; or of going to the restaurant – but without going in for a meal.

d   **auf** + *accusative* is used in a few fixed phrases such as:

> Ich gehe **auf die Toilette**.
> I'm going **to the toilet**.
>
> Wir fahren **aufs Land**.
> We're going **to the country(side)**.

3.9   Genitive

The genitive is the least common of the four German cases. It almost always corresponds to the meaning *of*:

> Hans ist der Sohn **eines spanischen Kellners**.
> Hans is the son **of a Spanish waiter**.
>
> die Zerstörung **der Umwelt**
> the destruction **of the environment**

German normally uses the genitive even where English uses *'s* instead of the word *of*:

Das ist das Auto **meines Vaters.**
That is **my father's car.** [= the car **of my father**]

The exception is when a person is referred to by name, including pet names such as **Mama** and **Papa.** Then **-s** is added to the name. (There is no apostrophe.)

Das ist Papa**s** Auto.
That is Dad**'s** car.

Das ist Frau Schmidt**s** Auto.
That is Frau Schmidt**'s** car.

Das ist Herr**n** Schmidts Auto. [See 1.6.]
That is Herr Schmidt**'s** car.

Genitive forms always involve the endings **-es** (m. and neut. sing.) or **-er** (f. sing. and pl. for all genders) on markers. Remember that masculine and neuter singular nouns add **-s** or **-es** in the genitive. Generally, short words add **-es** and longer words add **-s**, but this is not a strict rule. (See also 1.5 and 1.6.)

ein Foto **des** Kindes/Kinds   *a photo **of the** child*
ein Foto **des** Bahnhofs   *a photo **of the** railway station*

Avoiding the genitive

In conversation, the genitive can seem stilted and old-fashioned. It is often avoided and replaced by **von** + *dative*:

Das ist das Auto **von meinem Vater.**
(= Das ist das Auto **meines Vaters.**)
That is **my father's** car.

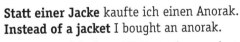

3.10 Prepositions with the genitive

There are four common prepositions with the genitive that you should know:

statt	*instead of*
trotz	*in spite of*
während	*during*
wegen	*because of*

Statt einer Jacke kaufte ich einen Anorak.
Instead of a jacket I bought an anorak.

Trotz des schlechten Wetters gingen wir schwimmen.
In spite of the bad weather, we went swimming.

Während der Ferien arbeitete ich bei der Post.
During the holidays I worked for the post office.

Wegen des Nebels mussten wir sehr langsam fahren.
Because of the fog, we had to drive very slowly.

3.11   Distinguishing prepositions, adverbs and conjunctions: *before* and *after*

English speakers who learn German often get confused by the various words for *before* (**vor, vorher, bevor**) and *after* (**nach, nachher, nachdem**).

a   **vor** and **nach** are prepositions. They occur before nouns or pronouns:

Ich wasche mich **vor dem Frühstück**.
I have a wash **before breakfast**.

Nach dem Film gehen wir essen.
After the film, we'll go for a meal.

Nach Ihnen!
After you!

b   **vorher** and **nachher** are adverbs of time. They mean *beforehand* and *afterwards*:

Wir gehen ins Kino, aber **vorher** gehen wir essen.
We'll go to the cinema, but **before(hand)** we'll go for a meal.

Wir gehen einkaufen, und **nachher** gehen wir schwimmen.
We'll go shopping, and **afterwards** we'll go swimming.

c   **bevor** and **nachdem** are conjunctions. They link two clauses (see 9.3 and 9.8).

Bevor ich meine Hausaufgaben mache, esse ich zu Abend.
Before I do my homework, I have my evening meal.

Nachdem ich mich gewaschen hatte, trocknete ich mich ab.
After I had had a wash, I dried myself.

4 Pronouns

Many pronouns are covered in other parts of the *Handbook*. For example, *question words* are covered in Chapter 5; *relative pronouns* are covered in 9.9.

4.1 What is a pronoun?

Pronouns are short words which we use in place of nouns. They are a form of shorthand to help us avoid repetition. Look at these two sentences:

Alison is eighteen. **Alison** lives in London and works in a bank.

They are obviously repetitious as they stand. We can improve them by using the pronoun *she* to replace *Alison* in the second sentence:

Alison is eighteen. **She** lives in London and works in a bank.

She is only one of many pronouns. In these further examples, the pronouns are emphasised in bold type:

I'd like you to meet Martin. **He** comes from Germany.
My car's gone! I think **it**'s been stolen!
I'll take you swimming. Would you like **that**?
Do you sell street maps? Good, I'd like **one**, please.

4.2 Personal pronouns

As the name suggests, these are pronouns which refer to people. (In fact, they can also refer to *things* – see 4.4.) German pronouns can occur in various cases, in a similar way to nouns. For details of the cases and their uses, see Chapter 3. The following examples show the German pronoun for *he* in its various cases:

Hast du Jochen gesehen?
Have you seen Jochen?

Wo ist **er**?
Where is **he**?

Hast du **ihn** gesehen?
Have you seen **him**?

Ich soll mit **ihm** Tennis spielen.
I'm supposed to be playing tennis with **him**.

er is nominative, **ihn** is accusative and **ihm** is dative.

The following table shows all the personal pronouns in nominative, accusative and dative. Genitive pronouns are not shown here because they are very rarely used.

The right-hand side shows the markers **mein**, **dein**, etc. (equivalents of *my*, *your*, etc.) to help you distinguish them from the pronouns. Take care on this point (see also 2.7).

	nom.	acc.	dat.	marker	
I, me	ich	mich	mir	mein	*my*
you	du	dich	dir	dein	*your*
he, him, it	er	ihn	ihm	sein	*his, its*
she, her, it	sie	sie	ihr	ihr	*her, its*
it	es	es	ihm	sein	*its*
we, us	wir	uns	uns	unser	*our*
you	ihr	euch	euch	euer	*your*
you	Sie	Sie	Ihnen	Ihr	*your*
they, them	sie	sie	ihnen	ihr	*their*

You will notice that there are three sets of pronouns corresponding to *you*, and these are explained in the next section (4.3). The pronouns for *he, she* and *it* are explained in 4.4.

man

The pronoun **man** means *one* (as in *One has to do one's best*), and can refer to either sex. *one* is often associated with upper-class speech in English, but **man** is freely used by everyone who speaks German. In English we often say *you* or *they* instead. Do not carry this over into your German – use **man** instead.

> Was **macht man** in dieser Situation?
> What **does one do** / What **do you do** in this situation?

> **Man sagt**, dass Portugal sehr schön ist.
> **They say** that Portugal is very beautiful.

The verb forms used are the same as those used with **er/sie/es**.

> The accusative of **man** is **einen**, the dative is **einem** and the possessive (*one's*) is **sein**, but these forms are not very common.

 Do not confuse **man** with **der Mann**.

4.3 *du, ihr* or *Sie*?

All three of these pronouns mean *you*.

4.3a *du*

Use **du** (and **dich, dir, dein** – see the table in 4.2) when speaking to any one person whom you address by first name. Children and teenagers automatically use **du** to each other, whether they are already friends or not. **du** is also always used when speaking to relatives. In letter-writing, **du, dich, dir** and **dein** are sometimes still written with a capital letter, but this is no longer compulsory.

> Wie alt bist **du**, Beate?
> How old are **you**, Beate?

Kann ich **dich** morgen besuchen?
Can I visit **you** tomorrow?

Wie geht es **dir**? [See 10.30d.]
How are **you**?

Wie ist **deine** Adresse?
What's **your** address?

4.3b *ihr*

Use **ihr** (and **euch**, **euer** – see the table in 4.2) when speaking to any two or more people to whom you would say **du**. **ihr** is simply the plural of **du**. **ihr** is also used when speaking to a mixture of people to whom you say **du** and **Sie**. In letter-writing, **ihr**, **euch** and **euer** are sometimes still written with a capital letter, but this is no longer compulsory.

Wie alt seid **ihr**, Beate und Rolf?
How old are **you**, Beate and Rolf?

Kann ich **euch** morgen besuchen?
Can I visit **you** tomorrow?

Wie geht es **euch**?
How are **you** [= you two / you all]?

Wie ist **euere/eure** Adresse?
What's **your** address?

4.3c *Sie*

Use **Sie** (and **Ihnen**, **Ihr** – see the table in 4.2) when speaking to any person or people with whom you are not on first-name terms. This means that you use **Sie** when speaking to adult strangers and other adults in positions of authority (such as teachers or policemen). These are all people whom you address as **Herr** (*Mr*), **Frau** (*Mrs* or *Ms*) or **Fräulein** (*Miss*). **Sie**, **Ihnen** and **Ihr** must *always* be written with a capital letter.

Wie alt sind **Sie**, Herr Schmidt?
How old are **you**, Herr Schmidt?

Kann ich **Sie** morgen besuchen?
Can I visit **you** tomorrow?

Wie geht es **Ihnen**?
How are **you**?

Wie ist **Ihre** Adresse?
What's **your** address?

4.4 How to use *er*, *sie* and *es*

These three pronouns (and their accusative, dative and marker forms – see 4.2) do not correspond exactly to the English pronouns *he*, *she* and *it*. This is because things as well as people have genders in German (see 1.2).

- **er** refers to any masculine noun
- **sie** refers to any feminine noun
- **es** refers to neuter nouns*

*sie is very often used to refer back to *das* **Mädchen**, and always to refer back to *das* **Fräulein**.

Ist das **dein neuer Volkswagen? Er** ist sehr schön. Wann hast
   du **ihn** gekauft?
Is that **your new Volkswagen? It's** very nice. When did you buy **it**?

Ist das **deine neue Jacke? Sie** ist sehr schön. Wann hast du **sie** gekauft?
Is that **your new jacket? It's** very nice. When did you buy **it**?

Ist das **dein neues Fahrrad? Es** ist sehr schön. Wann hast du **es** gekauft?
Is that **your new bike? It's** very nice. When did you buy **it**?

 Beware of the common mistake of using **es** when referring to masculine or
feminine nouns.

4.5   Ways of expressing *this* and *that*

a   **das** is the most general word, and it is used for both *this* and *that*:

   Was ist **das**?
   What's **this/that**?

   Das macht Spaß!
   This/that is fun!

   Das ist nett von dir.
   That's nice of you.

When referring back to a specific noun which has been mentioned previously,
use **dieser/diese/dieses** for *this* and **der/die/das** for *that*.

b   **dieser/diese/dieses**. For details of the endings used here, see 2.5.

   Ich möchte einen neuen Pullover. **Dieser** ist schön, aber **diese**
      sind schöner.
   I'd like a new pullover. **This (one)** is nice, but **these (ones)** are nicer.

c   **der/die/das** can be used as pronouns to mean *that*, as well as the usual
meaning of *the*. The endings are as shown in 2.4, except for the dative plural,
which is **denen** instead of **den**.

   Ich möchte einen neuen Pullover. **Der** ist schön, aber **die** sind schöner.
   I'd like a new pullover. **That (one)** is nice, but **those (ones)** are nicer.

4.6   *das* or *dass*?

 das and **dass** both correspond to *that* in English.

One use of **das** is described above in 4.5:

   Das ist ein Foto von meiner Mutter.
   That's a photo of my mother.

das can also be a relative pronoun meaning *that* or *which* (see 9.9):

   Das Fahrrad, das ich gekauft habe, hat viel Geld gekostet.
   The bike **that** [= **which**] I have bought cost a lot of money.

dass is a conjunction which opens subordinate clauses (see 9.8):

> Peter sagt, **dass** er mitkommen will.
> Peter says **that** he wants to come along.

> Jana ist so glücklich, **dass** sie die ganze Zeit lacht.
> Jana is so happy **that** she laughs all the time.

4.7 *einer/eine/eines* as pronouns

You already know the marker **ein/eine/ein** (see 2.6). There is also a pronoun with slightly different endings, **einer/eine/eines**:

	m.	f.	neut.
nom.	**einer**	eine	**eines***
acc.	einen	eine	**eines***
gen.	eines	einer	eines
dat.	einem	einer	einem

*In conversation often shortened to **eins**.

You will notice that most of the table is the same as that for the marker **ein/eine/ein**. The forms which are different are emphasised in bold type in the table. Here is an example:

> Da sind die zwei Jungen. **Einer** heißt Holger, und der andere heißt Roland.
> There are the two boys. **One** is called Holger and the other is called Roland.

> *one of the ...*
>
> **einer/eine/eines** is often used in this way:
>
> > **Einer der Jungen** stürzte von seinem Fahrrad.
> > **One of the** boys fell off his bike.
>
> **einer** is nominative, the subject of the verb **stürzte**. **der Jungen** is genitive plural: *of the boys*.

4.8 How to say *mine, yours, his, hers,* etc.

These pronouns are based on the markers **mein**, **dein**, **sein**, etc. (see 2.7 and 4.2), but with the same endings as those used on the pronoun **einer/eine/eines** in 4.7:

- Wo sind unsere Koffer?
- Da ist **meiner**, und hier ist **deiner**.

4.9 *da-* with prepositions: *davon, darin,* etc.

When in English *it* or *them* follow prepositions, and refer to things and not people, in German **da-** is used instead of the usual pronoun. Study these examples:

Das ist ein Foto von meinem Bruder.	--->	Das ist ein Foto **von ihm**.
This is a photo of my brother.	--->	This is a photo **of him**.
Das ist ein Foto von meinem VW-Polo.	--->	Das ist ein Foto **davon**.
This is a photo of my VW Polo.	--->	This is a photo **of it**.

This does not depend on gender (both the brother and the VW Polo are masculine in German), but on the fact that the brother is a person and the car is a thing. The system with **da-** can be used for plural things, too:

Das ist ein Foto von meinen Pflanzen.	--->	Das ist ein Foto **davon**.
This is a photo of my plants.	--->	This is a photo of **them**.

da- can be added to most prepositions. When the preposition starts with a vowel, we add **dar-**:

Mein Name war in meinem Mantel.	--->	Mein Name war **darin**.
My name was in my overcoat.	--->	My name was **in it**.

4.10   Omission of pronouns: verbs with the prefix *mit-*

With verbs such as **mitkommen**, **mitgehen**, **mitfahren** and **mitnehmen**, German does not need the pronoun that we always put in in English:

Kommst du **mit**?
Are you coming **with me/us**?

Ich will **mit**gehen.
I want to go **with you/him/them**, etc.

Ich bin **mit**gefahren.
I went with **you/her/them**, etc.

Können Sie mich **mit**nehmen?
Can you take me **with you**? [i.e. Can you give me a lift?]

4.11   How to say *nothing new, something interesting*, etc.

Ich habe **nichts Neues** gekauft.
I bought **nothing new**.

Hat er **etwas Interessantes** gesagt?
Did he say **anything interesting**?

Haben Sie **etwas Billigeres**?
Have you **anything cheaper**?

NOTE that the adjective is given a capital letter and the ending **-es**.

After **alles**, the adjective ends in **-e**:

Ich wünsche dir **alles Gute**!
I wish you **all the best**!

4.12 Other common pronouns

4.12a *some* and *any*

- Singular: **etwas**
- Plural: **einige** also: **welche**

> Wir haben Salat da. Möchtest du **etwas**?
> We have some salad here. Would you like **some**?

> Wir haben Kartoffelchips da. Möchtest du **einige/welche**?
> We have some crisps here. Would you like **some**?

See also 2.10.

4.12b *beide* and *die beiden*

These mean *both* or *the two of them*.

> Anna und Jörg gingen **beide** ins Kino.
> Anna and Jörg **both** went to the cinema.

> **Die beiden** wollten den neuen James-Bond-Film sehen.
> **The two of them** wanted to see the new James Bond film.

4.12c *alles* and *alle*

- **alles** is *singular* and means *everything*. The verb must be *singular*.
- **alle** is *plural* and means *everybody*. The verb must be *plural*.

> Wir wollten in Zürich einkaufen, aber **alles war** viel zu teuer.
> We wanted to go shopping in Zürich but **everything was** much
>   too expensive.

> Morgen fahre ich mit meiner Klasse nach Köln. **Alle sind** sehr aufgeregt.
> Tomorrow I'm going to Cologne with my class. **Everybody is** very excited.

5 Questions

Study these examples of typical German questions:

Hast du Geschwister?
Have you any brothers or sisters?

Arbeitest du in deiner Freizeit?
Do you work in your free time?

Arbeitet dein Bruder?
Does your brother work?

These are all questions which can be answered simply by **Ja** or **Nein**. They are made by turning the verb and its subject round, so that the verb starts the sentence (**Hast? Arbeitest? Arbeitet?**). English often brings in the verb *do* for this type of question (look at the English translations of the second and third of these examples: *Do you work?, Does your brother work?*). German does *not* do this.

Here are some more examples of typical German questions:

Wie heißt du?
What's your name?

Wo wohnst du?
Where do you live?

Was liest du?
What are you reading?

Wann kommt der Bus?
When does the bus come?

These questions are made in a similar way. NOTE that German never uses any equivalent of the verb *do* to help form the question. They start with special question words (**Wie? Wo? Was? Wann?**).

Here is a list of the question words you need to know:

was?	*what?*
wo?	*where?*
wer?	*who?* (nom.)
wen?	*who? whom?* (acc.)
wem?	*whom? to whom?* (dat.)
wessen?	*whose?*
warum?	*why?*
wieso?	*why? (how come?)*
wozu?	*what . . . for? (for what purpose?)*
wohin?	*where (to)?*
woher?	*where . . . from?*
wann?	*when?*
wie?	*how? (sometimes = what?)*

wieviel?	*how much?*
wie viele?	*how many?*
wie lange?	*how long?*
was für?	*what kind of?*
womit?	*with what?*
wovon?	*of/from what?*
worauf?	*on what?*

 wo? = *where?* and **wer?** = *who?*

a **womit, wovon, worauf**, etc. are formed by adding **wo-** to prepositions (**wor-** is added if the preposition starts with a vowel).

> **Womit** hast du das Brot geschnitten?
> **What** did you cut the bread **with**? [**With what** did you cut the bread?]

b **wessen** (*whose*)

> **Wessen** Schal ist das?
> **Whose** scarf is that?

In conversation, **wessen** is usually avoided. This example becomes:

> Wem gehört der Schal?
> To whom does that scarf belong? / Who does that scarf belong to?

c **was für?** (*What kind of?*)
was für is not followed by the accusative you would expect after **für**, unless the noun is the direct object of the question.

> Was für **ein** Schrank ist das?
> What kind of a cupboard is that?

> Was für **einen** Schrank hast du?
> What kind of a cupboard have you got?

6 Numbers and amounts

6.1 Numbers

0	null	21	einundzwanzig (**eins** drops its **s**)
1	eins	22	zweiundzwanzig
2	zwei (on telephone, radio, etc. often **zwo**)	26	sech**s**undzwanzig
3	drei	27	sieb**en**undzwanzig
4	vier	30	dreißig (**dreißig** has **ß** and not **z**)
5	fünf	40	vierzig
6	sechs	50	fünfzig
7	sieben	60	sechzig (**sechs** drops its **s**)
8	acht	70	siebzig (**sieben** drops its **en**)
9	neun	80	achtzig
10	zehn	90	neunzig
11	elf	100	hundert (more usual than **ein**hundert)
12	zwölf	101	hunderteins
13	dreizehn	125	hundertfünfundzwanzig
14	vierzehn	200	zweihundert
15	fünfzehn	600	sech**s**hundert
16	sechzehn (**sechs** drops its **s**)	700	sieb**en**hundert
17	siebzehn (**sieben** drops its **en**)	1000	tausend (more usual than **ein**tausend)
18	achtzehn		
19	neunzehn		
20	zwanzig		

3456	dreitausendvierhundertsechsundfünfzig
1999	neunzehnhundertneunundneunzig (the year)
2000	zweitausend
2001	zweitausendeins
1 000 000	eine Million

Points to remember

a The form **eins** is used when counting, and in mathematics:

> Seite **eins**   *page one*
> zwei und **eins** ist drei   *2 + 1 = 3*

When the German equivalent of *one* comes before a noun, the normal marker endings are used (see 2.6).

> Ich habe nur **einen** Bruder.
> I have only **one** brother.

b **Arithmetic**

zwei und drei ist fünf	sechs weniger vier ist zwei
2 + 3 = 5	6 − 4 = 2
elf mal eins ist elf	zehn durch fünf ist zwei
11 × 1 = 11	10 : 5 = 2

The last sum here shows the German division sign. It is usually **:** and not **÷**.

c **Telephone numbers**

Telephone numbers are often spoken in pairs, like this:

Meine Telefonnummer ist fünf, sechsundzwanzig, null acht.
My telephone number is 5 26 08.

d **Years**

NOTE that German does not use the word *in* in sentences such as this:

Ich bin 1986 geboren. (Ich bin neunzehnhundertsechsundachtzig geboren.)
I was born **in** 1986.

6.2 Fractions and decimals

6.2a Fractions

$\frac{1}{2}$	(ein) halb	$\frac{3}{4}$	drei Viertel
$\frac{1}{3}$	ein Drittel	$1\frac{1}{2}$	eineinhalb (or the special word: anderthalb)
$\frac{1}{4}$	ein Viertel	$2\frac{1}{2}$	zweieinhalb

half

These examples show the most common forms:

ein halbes Pfund, bitte!	*half a pound, please!*
eine halbe Stunde später	*half an hour later*

You may also meet the noun **die Hälfte**:

Ich aß die **Hälfte des Brötchens**.
I ate **half (of) the roll**.

6.2b Decimals

German uses a comma where English uses a decimal point:

1,5 einskommafünf   *1.5 one point five*

6.3 How to say *once, twice, three times*, etc.

These words are very easy, as these examples show:

Kaviar habe ich nur **einmal** gegessen.
I've only eaten caviar **once**.

Frank hat mich **zweimal** besucht.
Frank visited me **twice**.

Ich war schon **dreimal** in Deutschland.
I've been to Germany **three** times.

6.4   How to say *first, second, third*, etc.

These numbers are really adjectives (e.g. *the **first** girl, the **second** house*), and they therefore need normal adjective endings in German.

> Der **erste** Monat ist Januar.
> The **first** month is January.

> Marianne war das **zweite** Mädchen.
> Marianne was the **second** girl.

> Der Golf ist mein **drittes** Auto.
> The Golf is my **third** car.

The others, up to *tenth*, are:

> der vierte
> der fünfte
> der sechste
> der siebte (OR: der siebente)
> der achte (NOTE: only one **t**)
> der neunte
> der zehnte

This system of adding **-te** to the number continues up to and including *nineteenth* (**der neunzehnte**). For all numbers after *nineteenth*, **-ste** must be added:

> der zwanzigste, der einundzwanzigste, der hundertste

When writing in figures, do it like this:

> der **1.** Preis   *1st prize*

The full stop is compulsory. These numbers occur most often in dates (see 6.5).

6.5   Dates

Here are some examples:

> Der wievielte ist heute?
> What's the date today?

> Heute ist **der fünfte März.**
> Today is **the fifth of March.**

> Heute ist **der 5. März.**
> Today is **the 5th of March.**

The key example is the second one. **der fünfte** is used as a short way of saying **der fünfte Tag** (*the fifth day*). That is why a masculine marker is used. The **-e** ending on **fünfte** is a normal adjective ending (see 2.4).

Dating letters

For the date at the top of a letter, the accusative is used:

> Hannover, den 4. Juni

This is read as: 'Hannover, den **vierten** Juni.' (See also 7.6.)

Birthdays

This table shows how to say when your (or someone else's) birthday is:

| Ich habe
Mein Bruder hat
Meine Schwester
hat (usw.)

*For details of the
numbers used here,
see 6.4.* | **am** | ersten
zweiten
dritten
vierten
fünften
sechsten
siebten
achten
neunten
(usw.)
neunzehnten
zwanzigsten
einundzwanzigsten
(usw.)
dreißigsten
einunddreißigsten | Januar
Februar
März
April
Mai
Juni
Juli
August
September
Oktober
November
Dezember | **Geburtstag** |

 NOTE that the German and English versions do not correspond word for word!

Ich habe am einunddreißigsten Juli Geburtstag.
My birthday is (on) the 31st of July.

from ... to ...

Ich bleibe **vom** fünft**en bis zum** zwölft**en** September.
I'm staying **from the** fifth **to the** twelfth of September.

6.6   Quantities and money

6.6a   Quantities

Ich kaufe zwei **Kilo** Zucker.
I'm buying two **kilos of** sugar.

Er trank drei **Liter** Bier.
He drank three **litres of** beer.

Ich trank drei **Glas** Cola.
I drank three **glasses of** cola.

In this kind of expression, the words which show a quantity (e.g. **Kilo**, **Liter**, **Glas**, **Pfund**, etc.) do not change to show the plural. They are left in their singular form.

EXCEPTIONS:
zwei Tasse**n** Tee, zwei Flasche**n** Wein

English includes the word *of* (e.g. *two kilos **of** sugar*). The German expressions do not include any word for *of*.

6.6b Money

The Euro

der Euro, der Cent

> Das kostet fünf Cent.
> einen Euro.
> einen Euro zwanzig.
> zwei Euro.

NOTE that neither **Euro** nor **Cent** shows any change in the plural after a number.

Traditional German currency

die Mark, der Pfennig

> Das kostet fünf Pfennig. (5Pf. / –,05 Pf.)
> eine Mark. (DM 1,–)
> eine Mark zwanzig. (DM 1,20)
> zwei Mark. (DM 2,–)

NOTE that neither **Mark** nor **Pfennig** shows any change in the plural after a number.

The word *Deutschmark* does not exist in German. You will sometimes find the full name **Deutsche Mark**, and the shortened form **D-Mark**. Note the special name for the ten-Pfennig piece: **der Groschen (-)**.

Traditional Austrian currency

der Schilling – **ein Schilling, zwei Schilling.**
1 Schilling = 100 **Groschen.**

Switzerland

Switzerland has **Franken**, divided into 100 **Rappen** (**der Franken (-)**, **der Rappen (-)**).

Other currencies

Also note **der Dollar, das Pfund, der Penny** (plural: **Pence**).

> Ein Hamburger kostet einen Dollar fünfzig / neunzig Pence.
> Diese Vase kostet zwanzig Dollar fünfzig / zwanzig Pfund fünfzig.

As with other currency words, these words show no change in the plural after a number.

6.6c Quantities and money

> Die Kartoffeln kosten fünfzig Cent **das** Kilo.
> The potatoes cost fifty cents **a** kilo.

> Die Butter kostet sechs Franken **das** Pfund.
> The butter costs six francs **per** pound.

> Die Bleistifte kosten zwanzig Cent **das** Stück.
> The pencils cost twenty cents **each**.

In this kind of sentence, German uses words for *the*, where in English we usually use *a* or *per*.

6.7   Measurements

Ich wiege fünfundsechzig Kilo.
I weigh 65 kilos.

Ich bin ein Meter siebzig groß.
My height is 1.70 metres.

Mein Zimmer ist vier Meter lang und drei Meter breit.
My room is four metres long and three metres wide.

Mein Zimmer ist vier mal drei.
My room is four by three (metres).

The use of the accusative in measurements

The accusative is needed in expressions such as these:

Das Auto ist erst **einen Monat** alt.
The car is only **one month** old.

Diese Straße ist **einen Kilometer** lang.
This road is **one kilometre** long.

For details of the accusative, see 3.3.

7 Time

7.1 Introduction

There is an enormous variety of time expressions, and they cannot all be listed here. Dates are dealt with in 6.5. For *before* and *after*, see 3.11.

7.2 Clock time

Wie spät ist es? / Wieviel Uhr ist es?
What time is it?

7.2a The everyday method

Es ist zwei Uhr.

Es ist fünf nach zwei.

Es ist zehn nach zwei.

Es ist Viertel nach zwei.

Es ist zwanzig nach zwei.

Es ist fünf vor halb drei.

Es ist halb drei.

Es ist fünf nach halb drei.

Es ist zwanzig vor drei.

Es ist Viertel vor drei.

Es ist zehn vor drei.

Es ist fünf vor drei.

one o'clock	**ein** Uhr
five past one (etc.)	fünf nach **eins** (usw.)

Twenty-five past, half past and *twenty-five to* are the times which, in German, are most different from the English method of telling the time. English looks back to the previous hour (*half past* **two**), whereas German looks ahead to the next hour (**halb** *drei*). Twenty-five past is regarded as five minutes before the half hour (*twenty-five past two* – **fünf vor halb drei**), and twenty-five to is regarded as five minutes after the half hour (*twenty-five to three* – **fünf nach halb drei**).

at + clock time

To say *at* a certain time, German uses **um**:

Ich stehe **um** sieben Uhr auf.
I get up **at** seven o'clock.

at about + clock time

To give an approximate time in German, use **gegen**:

Ich stehe **gegen** sieben Uhr auf.
I get up (**at**) **about** seven o'clock.

Second, minute and *hour*

die Sekunde (-n)	*second*
die Minute (-n)	*minute*
die Stunde (-n)	*hour*

Do not confuse **Stunde** and **Uhr**. **Stunde** means *hour*, **Uhr** means *clock* and *o'clock*.

7.2b   The 24-hour clock

This is much easier than the everyday method. It is used a lot more in German-speaking countries than in English-speaking ones. It is quite often used even in conversation. Here are some examples which show how to express times on the 24-hour clock:

Es ist zwei Uhr.	*It is 02.00 hours (2 am).*
Es ist vierzehn Uhr.	*It is 14.00 hours (2 pm).*
Es ist sechzehn Uhr fünf.	*It is 16.05 (4.05 pm).*
Es ist achtzehn Uhr fünfundzwanzig.	*It is 18.25 (6.25 pm).*

In figures, write it like this:

Es ist 2 Uhr.
Es ist 14 Uhr.
Es ist 16.05 Uhr.
Es ist 18.25 Uhr.
usw.

The 24-hour clock is especially used when talking about travel arrangements:

Der Zug fährt **um zwanzig Uhr** ab.
The train leaves at **8 pm**.

7.3   *for* + time

In English we often use phrases involving *for* with an expression of time:

Last night I watched TV **for two hours**.
Tomorrow I'm going to Germany **for ten days**.
I have been learning German **for three years**.

These three examples correspond to the three different German ways of dealing with this type of expression.

a   In most instances, there is no equivalent of the English *for*:

Gestern Abend sah ich **zwei Stunden** fern.
Last night I watched TV **for two hours**.

It is optional to add the word **lang**:

Gestern Abend sah ich **zwei Stunden lang** fern.

b When talking about future plans, **für** + *accusative* is used:

> Morgen fahre ich **für zehn Tage** nach Deutschland.
> Tomorrow I'm going to Germany **for ten days**.

c To show that an activity started in the past and *continues* up to the time you are talking about, German uses **seit** + *dative*. The tenses used are different from those used in English, which generally include the words *have been* or *had been*. This pair of sentences should make the point clear:

> Ich **lerne seit drei Jahren** Deutsch.
> I **have been learning** German **for three years**.

The German sentence literally says 'I am learning German since three years' – the reason for the present tense being that I am still learning German *now*, in the present.

The sentence can be transferred into the past:

> Ich **lernte seit drei Jahren** Deutsch, als ich nach Berlin fuhr.
> I **had been learning** German **for three years** when I went to Berlin.

The two pairs of examples above show the two German tenses that can be used in this type of sentence – *present* and *simple past*.

> EXCEPTION: *negative* sentences require the *perfect* or *pluperfect*:
>
> > Ich **habe** ihn **seit drei Jahren** nicht mehr **gesehen**.
> > I **have** not **seen** him **for three years**.
>
> The point here is that the activity does *not* continue up to the present.

7.4 How to say *when*: *wann, als* and *wenn*

  These often cause confusion!

a **wann** is a question word (see Chapter 5), and must be used whenever a question is involved. This includes reported questions (see 10.38b).

> **Wann** kommst du nach Deutschland?
> **When** are you coming to Germany?

> Ich fragte den Schaffner, **wann** der Zug in Bonn ankommen würde.
> I asked the ticket inspector **when** the train would arrive in Bonn.

> Ich weiß nicht, **wann** der Film beginnt.
> I don't know **when** the film begins.

b For talking about *a single event in a story or narrative sequence*, you must use **als**:

> **Als** ich in der Schule ankam, war es schon Viertel nach neun.
> **When** I arrived at school, it was already quarter past nine.

c Other uses of *when* in English are covered by the German word **wenn**:

> **Wenn** Renate ankommt, gehen wir alle ins Theater.
> **When** Renate arrives, we'll all go to the theatre.

When talking about the past, **wenn** means *whenever*:

Wenn ich in der Schule ankam, spielte ich immer Fußball mit Udo.
When(ever) I arrived at school, I always used to play football with Udo.

als and **wenn** are conjunctions which introduce subordinate clauses. For more details, see 9.8.

7.5 How to pinpoint times: *in/on/at* + time

The following sections explain various possibilities.

7.5a Years

German simply gives the year. It is wrong to use **in** ...

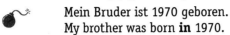

Mein Bruder ist 1970 geboren.
My brother was born **in** 1970.

7.5b Months and seasons

Use **im**:

Ich habe **im Januar** Geburtstag.
My birthday is **in January**.

Im Winter gehe ich Skilaufen.
In winter I go skiing.

The seasons:

der Frühling *spring*
der Sommer *summer*
der Herbst *autumn*
der Winter *winter*

For the months, see 6.5.

7.5c Days and parts of days

Use **am** + the day (or part of the day) for one occasion. For several occasions, just add **-s** to the day (or part of the day).

Am Samstag gingen wir aus.
On Saturday, we went out.

Wir gingen **samstags** aus.
We went out **on Saturdays**.

NOTE that in the second example, **samstags** has a small letter.

Similarly:

am Montag / montags   *on Monday / Mondays*
am Dienstag / dienstags   *on Tuesday / Tuesdays*

The days of the week, starting with *Sunday,* are:

Sonntag, Montag, Dienstag, Mittwoch, Donnerstag, Freitag, Samstag (or, in North Germany: **Sonnabend**).

All these are masculine.

Parts of the day are treated in the same way:

am Morgen / morgens	*in the morning / mornings*
am Vormittag / vormittags	*in the morning / mornings*
am Nachmittag / nachmittags	*in the afternoon / afternoons*
am Abend / abends	*in the evening / evenings*

All these parts of the day are masculine. **die Nacht** is treated slightly differently:

in der Nacht / nachts	*in the night / at night*

The days and parts of days can be combined, like this:

am Montagabend /montagabends	*on Monday evening / evenings*

Also:

morgens um 10 Uhr	*at 10 o'clock in the morning*
um 8 Uhr abends	*at 8 o'clock in the evening*

7.5d *this morning*, etc.

heute	*today*
heute Morgen	*this morning*
heute Abend	*this evening*
morgen	*tomorrow*
morgen Abend	*tomorrow evening*
übermorgen	*the day after tomorrow*
gestern	*yesterday*
gestern Morgen	*yesterday morning*
gestern Abend	*yesterday evening*
vorgestern	*the day before yesterday*

For *tomorrow morning*, say **morgen früh** (*not* ~~morgen Morgen!~~).

NOTE also:

am nächsten Tag	*(on) the next day*
am folgenden Tag	*(on) the following day*
am nächsten Morgen	*(on) the next morning*
usw.	*etc.*

7.5e How to say *one day*, *one morning*, etc.

The following fixed expressions use the genitive:

eines Tages	*one day*
eines Sonntags, usw.	*one Sunday, etc.*
eines Morgens	*one morning*
eines Abends	*one evening*
eines Nachts*	*one night*

*__eines Nachts__ is very odd – this genitive form looks masculine or neuter. In fact, **die Nacht** is feminine!

To say *one **fine** day* or *one **foggy November** morning*, change from genitive to **an** + dative:

an einem schönen Tag	*one fine day*
an einem nebligen Novembermorgen	*one foggy November morning*

7.6   The use of the accusative in time expressions

When there is no preposition involved and there is no reason to use any other case (as in 7.5.e), time expressions are put into the accusative. Of course, the accusative only shows up clearly with masculine nouns. The following example sentences show many of the commonest expressions:

Ich war **einen Tag** in Bonn.
I was in Bonn **for a day.**

Ich las **den ganzen Tag** (lang).
I read **all day** (long).

Sie arbeitet **die ganze Zeit.**
She works **all the / the whole time.**

Ich sehe **jeden Tag** fern.
I watch TV **every day.**

Sie geht **jeden Abend** aus.
She goes out **every night/evening.**

Wir fahren **jedes Jahr** nach Spanien.
We go to Spain **every year.**

Ich besuche ihn **jeden Monat.**
I visit him **every month.**

Sie kommt **nächsten Freitag.**
She's coming **next Friday.**

Sie kommt **nächste Woche.**
She's coming **next week.**

Sie kommt **nächstes Jahr.**
She's coming **next year.**

Ich war **letzten Montag** in London.
I was in London **last Monday.**

NOTE that we often say *night* in English when we really mean *evening*. This must be **Abend** in German.

> In German the accusative is used for the date in headings, for example in a letter:
> Hamburg, **den** 9. (= **neunten**) Mai
> For more on the accusative, see 3.4 and following sections.

7.7   Using *erst, zuerst, zunächst* and *erst mal*

erst is used in time expressions, where in English we would say *only* or *not until*:

Wir kamen **erst** gestern an.
We arrived **only** yesterday. / We did **not** arrive **until** yesterday.

Erst als das Telefon klingelte, wachte ich auf.
Only when / Not until the telephone rang did I wake up.

Er ist **erst** zehn Jahre alt.
He is **only** ten years old.

In the last example, the idea is not *not until* but *only ten years old so far*. In all these examples, **nur**, the usual word for *only* would be wrong.

zuerst is usually used for *first* meaning *at first* or *first of all*; **zunächst** can also be used but it is less common. In conversation, **erst mal** is often used for the first activity in a sequence.

> **Zuerst** gingen wir einkaufen.
> **First (of all)** we went shopping.

> Essen wir **zunächst** einmal, dann . . .
> Let's eat **first (of all)**, then . . .

> Ich will mich **erst mal** waschen, dann . . .
> **First (of all)** I want to have a wash, then . . .

7.8 How to express *ago*

Phrases which involve *ago* in English are expressed in German using **vor** + *dative*. (For other uses of **vor** + *dative*, see 3.7.)

> Der Zug fuhr **vor einer Stunde** ab.
> The train left **an hour ago**.

> Wir kamen **vor zwei Tagen** an.
> We arrived **two days ago**.

7.9 Other useful time expressions

These expressions are often used to begin sentences. When they are used in this way, the main verb must follow them immediately (see 9.4).

dann	*then*
einige Minuten später	*a few minutes later*
endlich	*at last*
gerade in diesem Moment	*just at that moment*
inzwischen	*meanwhile*
kurz danach	*shortly afterwards*
nach einer Weile	*after a while*
ohne Weiteres	*without further ado*
plötzlich	*suddenly*
schließlich	*finally*
währenddessen	*meanwhile*
zur Zeit	*at the moment*

<u>Yet more time expressions!</u>

bis jetzt	*up to now*
das nächste Mal	*next time*
das letzte Mal	*last time*
zum ersten Mal	*for the first time*
zum letzten Mal	*for the last time*
diesmal	*this time*
manchmal	*sometimes*
bald	*soon*
gleich	*very soon, straight away*
sofort	*immediately*
noch	*still*

immer noch	*still* (emphatic)
immer wieder	*over and over again*
immer	*always*
nie/niemals	*never*
stundenlang	*for hours* (*on end*)
tagelang	*for days* (*on end*)
rechtzeitig	*in time / on time*
oft	*often*
selten	*seldom, rarely*
Anfang Mai (usw.)	*at the beginning of May* (etc.)
Mitte Juni (usw.)	*in the middle of June* (etc.)
Ende Juli (usw.)	*at the end of July* (etc.)
zu Weihnachten	*at Christmas*
zu Ostern	*at Easter*

8 Particles

8.1 What is a particle?

A particle is something small. In German, particles are the small words such as **schon**, **da**, **doch**, etc. with which German-speakers love to 'sprinkle' their language. A particle can affect the meaning of a sentence in quite a subtle way.

8.2 *ja*

As well as being the word for *yes*, **ja** (often coming in the middle of a sentence) has a range of meanings such as *really, after all, of course*. It adds emphasis to what the speaker is saying and generally conveys the idea that the speaker expects the listener to agree with, or already know, what he or she is saying.

Ulli kann nicht Skilaufen gehen. Er ist ja krank.
Ulli cannot go skiing. He is ill (of course / after all).

Das ist ja interessant!
That's interesting! (isn't it?)

Du weißt ja, dass ich nicht schwimmen kann.
You know (of course) that I cannot swim.

8.3 *aber*

As a conjunction **aber** means *but*, and placed later in the sentence it often means *however*:

Jochen war sehr nervös; Jutta **aber** blieb ganz ruhig.
Jochen was very nervous; Jutta, **however**, remained quite calm.

The position of **aber** in this example shows an apparent exception to the 'verb second' rule (see 9.4).

As a particle **aber** can be used to add emphasis;

Das hat aber gut geschmeckt!
That really did taste good!

Das war aber dumm von dir!
That *was* stupid of you!

8.4   *doch*

doch can be a one-word answer, meaning *yes*, contradicting a negative idea:

> Maria kann kein Englisch, oder?   **Doch!**
> Maria can't speak English, can she?   **Yes!** [= Oh yes she can!]

Used after a command form (see 10.10), **doch** can help the speaker beg or encourage the listener to go along with what he or she is suggesting:

> Komm **doch** mit!
> **Go on**, come with us!

> Schrei **doch** nicht so!
> **Please** don't shout like that!

Often **doch** shows that the speaker is protesting slightly:

> Das ist **doch** unmöglich!
> **But** that's impossible!

OR appealing for the listener to agree with him or her – we sometimes say *after all* for this meaning in English:

> Jan kann nicht zur Schule gehen. Er ist **doch** krank!
> Jan cannot go to school. **After all**, he's ill!

doch can also mean *nevertheless, despite everything*:

> Die Hose war sehr teuer, aber ich habe sie **doch** gekauft.
> The trousers were very expensive, but I bought them **nevertheless**.

8.5   *mal*

mal ist short for **einmal**, which means *once*.

> Ich habe den Film schon **mal** / schon **einmal** gesehen.
> I've seen that film **once** already.

As a particle, it often means *just* or *just for once*. In this meaning, it is usually shortened in conversation from **einmal** to **mal**:

> Komm **mal** her!
> (**Just**) come here! [i.e. It's only a small thing I'm asking]

> Moment **mal**!
> **Just** a moment!

> Warst du schon **mal** in Deutschland?
> Have you **ever** been to Germany (once)?

nicht einmal and **nicht mal** mean *not even*:

> Die CD kostet zwanzig Mark, aber ich habe **nicht mal** / **nicht einmal** zwei Mark!
> The CD costs twenty Marks, but I haven**'t even** got two Marks!

8.6   *schon*

schon means *already*, but German speakers put it into sentences much more often than we say *already* in English.

> Es regnet **schon** wieder.
> It's started raining again (**already**).

> Ich verstehe **schon**!
> I understand! (You needn't tell me, I understand!)

> Das geht **schon**!
> It's all right!

8.7   *denn*

denn is often used in spoken questions, much as we use *then* in English:

> Wie alt bist du **denn**?
> How old are you (**then**)?

> Was ist **denn** los?
> What's the matter (**then**)?

denn is also often used as a conjunction meaning *for* in the sense of *because* (see 9.7).

 Do not confuse **denn** with **dann**, which means *then* in the sense of *after that* or *next*:

> Wir deckten den Tisch. **Dann** aßen wir zu Mittag.
> We laid the table. **Then** we had lunch.

8.8   *zwar*

The basic meaning of **zwar** is *admittedly*:

> Falk ist **zwar** ein sehr guter Schwimmer, aber Holger ist noch besser.
> Falk is a very good swimmer, **I admit**, but Holger is even better.

und zwar is used to add further details to what has already been said:

> Wir möchten zwei Tage bleiben, **und zwar** vom fünften bis zum siebten Juli.
> We should like to stay for two days, from the fifth to the seventh of
> July **to be precise**.

9 Word order and conjunctions

9.1 Word order: introduction

German word order is quite often different from English:

Nächstes Jahr besuche ich meine Freunde in Deutschland.

Next year I shall visit my friends in Germany.

Ich bleibe zu Hause, weil ich zu viele Hausaufgaben habe.

I'm staying at home, because I have too much homework.

The following sections explain the German system of word order.

9.2 Sentences and clauses

A sentence is made up of one or more *clauses*.

What is a clause?

A clause is a group of words that make sense together – normally there must be at least a subject and a verb:

Peter schwimmt.
Peter swims.

A clause can also be much longer. The first example in 9.1 above is also a sentence consisting of just one clause. However, a sentence can contain more than one clause. They may be simply added together, such as happens when **und** is put between them.

Ich mache meine Hausaufgaben **und** meine Mutter sieht fern.
I do my homework **and** my mother watches television.

For details of this type of sentence, see 9.7.

9.3 Main clauses and subordinate clauses

In 9.2 we saw how clauses can be 'added' together to form one longer sentence. However, this is not the only way of combining clauses. Look at this example:

Ulrike ist im Bett, weil sie krank ist.
Ulrike is in bed because she is ill.

This sentence consists of two clauses (separated in German by the comma).

Ulrike ist im Bett is the main part of the sentence here. It could be a sentence on its own. It is the main clause.

weil sie krank ist is a piece of extra information joined on to the main clause. It is not a sentence in its own right. This is called a subordinate clause.

The subordinate clause can be joined on to the beginning of the main clause as well as on to the end.

> Obwohl ich krank war, ging ich zur Schule.
> Although I was ill, I went to school.

Here the subordinate clause is **Obwohl ich krank war**, and it comes before the main clause. For details of this type of sentence, see 9.8.

9.4 Word order in main clauses: the 'verb second' rule

The most important word order rule in German language is the 'verb second' rule. According to this rule, *in a main clause, the main verb must be the second item in the clause*:

> Ich fuhr letztes Jahr nach Österreich.
> I went to Austria last year.

The verb here is **fuhr** (*went*). In both the German and the English sentences, it is the second item. The first item is the subject **ich** (*I*). We can, however, rearrange the word order of the sentence, like this:

> Letztes Jahr **fuhr ich** nach Österreich.
> Last year **I went** to Austria.

In this version of the sentence, the first item is **Letztes Jahr** (*Last year*). Note that an 'item' can consist of more than one word. In the German sentence the verb (**fuhr**) must follow the first item immediately. The subject (**ich**) is moved, so that it comes after the verb. The English sentence has different word order: *went* is the third item, after *Last year* and *I*.

One further rearrangement of the words in this sentence is possible – in German, but not in English:

> Nach Österreich **fuhr** ich letztes Jahr.

Now, **Nach Österreich** is the first item, but the verb (**fuhr**) is still the second item.

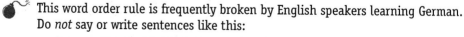 This word order rule is frequently broken by English speakers learning German. Do *not* say or write sentences like this:

> ~~Gestern Abend, ich bin in die Disko gegangen.~~

There should be no comma, and the sentence should read:

> Gestern Abend **bin** ich in die Disko gegangen.

The first item is **Gestern Abend**, then comes the verb **bin**, followed by the subject **ich**. This is a perfect-tense sentence, so part of the verb is at the end – **gegangen**. This is a feature of the perfect tense (see 10.17 and following sections). Often, there is an infinitive at the end:

Um sieben Uhr **muss** ich **aufstehen.**

Here, the main verb (**muss**) is the second item, as usual. There is also an infinitive at the end (**aufstehen**) (see 10.8).

<u>Words or phrases which can act as the 'first item' in the main clauses</u>

a The first item is very often the *subject*:

Wir gehen ins Schwimmbad.
We are going to the swimming-baths.
Mein alter Deutschlehrer hieß Smith.
My old German teacher was called Smith.

b The first item can be the *object*:

Den Briefträger biss der Hund.
The dog bit **the postman.**

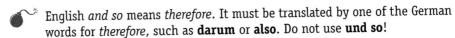

(See 3.1 for further explanation.)

c The first item can also be a *time expression*:

Dann kam ein Polizist an.
Then a policeman arrived.

Einige Minuten später fuhr der Zug ab.
A few minutes later the train left.

There are many time expressions which can be used in this way. Some of the commonest ones are listed in 7.9.

d The first item can be some other expression. Here are a few common ones which you will need to know:

glücklicherweise	*fortunately*
unglücklicherweise	*unfortunately*
leider	*unfortunately*
zum Glück	*fortunately*
darum	*and so, therefore*
deswegen/daher	*because of this, therefore*
also	*and so, therefore*

Here are some examples of these expressions in action:

Peter lief ins Kino. **Leider** hatte der Film schon angefangen.
Peter ran into the cinema. **Unfortunately** the film had already started.

Wir waren sehr müde, **darum/also** gingen wir sofort nach Hause.
We were very tired, **and so** we went home straight away.

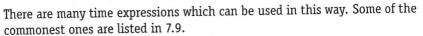 English *and so* means *therefore*. It must be translated by one of the German words for *therefore*, such as **darum** or **also**. Do not use **und so**!

English *so* often means *therefore*, too, and must be treated in the same way:

Ich musste Geld wechseln. **Darum** ging ich zur Bank.
I had to change some money. **So** I went to the bank.

All these 'first items' mean that the verb must follow immediately as the 'second item'!

<u>Words or phrases that cannot act as 'first item'</u>

a   **Ja** and **nein** at the beginning of a sentence do not count as the first item:

Ja, Petra **fährt** nach München.
Yes, Petra **is going** to Munich.

Nein, nächste Woche **kann** ich dich nicht besuchen.
No, next week I **can't** visit you.

Here, **Ja** and **Nein** do not count. The first items are **Petra** and **nächste Woche**. The verbs **fährt** and **kann** are the second items.

b   The same thing happens with anything else placed *before a comma at the beginning*, before the main sentence starts:

Markus, du **bleibst** hier, ja?
Markus, you**'re staying** here, aren't you?

Also, jetzt **können** wir essen!
Well then, now we **can** eat!

NOTE that this last example shows a different meaning of **also** from its meaning of *therefore* described earlier in this section.

c   **aber** meaning *however* can be placed between the first item and the verb:

Regine ging ins Theater. **Angela aber blieb** zu Hause.
Regine went to the theatre. **Angela, however, stayed** at home.

9.5   The 'time–manner–place' rule

According to this rule (often known as the 'TMP' rule), expressions of time, manner and place, when they occur next to each other in a sentence, must be placed in the order: time, manner, place.

a   Expressions of *time* include: **heute, nächste Woche**, etc. (see 7.5).

b   Expressions of *manner* include: **schnell, mit dem Bus, zu Fuß** (expressions of manner say *how* something is done).

c   Expressions of *place* include: **hier, dort, in die Stadt, in der Stadt**, etc.

Here are some sentences to show the TMP rule in action:

NOTE that English puts the words in a different order:

I go to school by bus every day.
Anna is going to Dortmund tomorrow.

9.6 The 'order of objects' rules

These are the word order rules for indirect and direct objects (for explanation of these, see 3.3. and 3.5).

Rule 1: the first rule is that, when both objects are nouns, the indirect (dative) comes before the direct (accusative):

	indirect object	direct object
Meine Mutter schenkte	**meinem Vater**	**einen neuen Regenschirm.**

My mother gave **my father a new umbrella.**

Rule 2: this rule says that a pronoun comes before a noun in the part of the sentence after the verb. This sometimes leads to the same word order as in the example above – if the pronoun represents the indirect object:

	indirect object	direct object
Meine Mutter schenkte	**ihm**	**einen neuen Regenschirm.**

My mother gave **him a new umbrella.**

But a pronoun still comes first, even if it is an accusative one that represents a direct object:

	direct object	indirect object
Meine Mutter schenkte	**ihn**	**meinem Vater.**

My mother gave **it to my father.**

Rule 3: when both objects are pronouns, the direct object (accusative) comes first:

	direct object	indirect object
Meine Mutter schenkte	**ihn**	**ihm.**

My mother gave **it to him.**

We can summarise these rules like this:

1 Two nouns: indirect object first.
2 Pronoun and noun: pronoun first.
3 Two pronouns: direct object first.

9.7 Sentences made up of two main clauses 'added' together: *und, aber,* etc.

The following five conjunctions link together two main clauses, without affecting the word order in any way:

und	*and*
aber*	*but*
denn	*for* (in the sense of *because*)
sondern*	*but*
oder	*or*

*For the difference between **aber** and **sondern**, see (a) below.

When these conjunctions are used, the 'verb second' rule applies to both clauses, in both halves of the sentence:

verb second   conjunction   verb second

Dieter ⌈hat⌉ ein Motorrad ⌈aber⌉ sein Bruder ⌈hat⌉ ein Auto.
Dieter has a motor-bike, but his brother has a car.

verb second   conjunction   verb second

Heute ⌈bleiben⌉ wir in Köln ⌈und⌉ morgen ⌈fahren⌉ wir nach Bonn.
Today we are staying in Cologne, and tomorrow we are going to Bonn.

 und, **aber**, **denn**, **sondern** and **oder** do not affect word order!

Points to remember

a **aber** is the usual word for *but*. However, **sondern** must be used when the second clause contradicts a negative statement in the first clause:

Heute abend sehen wir **nicht** fern, **sondern** wir gehen in die Disko.
Tonight we are **not** watching TV, **but** going to the disco.

Helga ist **nicht** müde, **sondern** krank.
Helga is **not** tired **but** ill.

b Sentences made up of two main clauses normally have a comma between the two halves of the sentence, though this is no longer compulsory.

NOTE that there is never a comma when there is only one subject for both clauses (e.g. **Klaudia** spielt Tennis und geht gern schwimmen).

9.8 Subordinate clauses – *Nebensätze*

Subordinate clauses are defined in 9.3.

In subordinate clauses in German, the verb goes to the end of the clause:

Ich kann nicht in Urlaub fahren, weil ich kein Geld **habe**.
I cannot go on holiday because I have no money.

weil ich kein Geld habe is a subordinate clause, starting with the *subordinating conjunction* **weil**. The verb **habe** is moved from its usual place (**ich** *habe* **kein Geld**) to the end of the clause.

The common subordinating conjunctions which you need to know are:

bevor	*before* (see 3.11)
damit	*so that*
dass	*that*
ob	*whether, if*
obwohl/obgleich	*although*
seitdem	*since*
sobald	*as soon as*
während	*while*
weil	*because*
wenn	*when*
als	*when* (see 7.4)

All these introduce subordinate clauses, in which the verb is sent to the end.

Ich gehe ins Kino, **wenn es** einen guten Film **gibt**.
I go to the cinema, **when there's** a good film.

Petra ging zur Fete, **obwohl/obgleich sie** viele Hausaufgaben **hatte**.
Petra went to the party, **although she had** a lot of homework.

Es ist schade, **dass du** nicht **mitkommen kannst**.
It is a pity **that you can't come** with us.

Es war sehr spät, **als wir angekommen sind**.
It was very late **when we arrived**.

The last two examples above show what happens when there are two verbs or when the verb is made up of more that one word:

du **kannst** nicht mitkommen ····⟩ … dass du nicht mitkommen **kannst**
wir **sind** angekommen ····⟩ … als wir angekommen **sind**

The two parts of a separable verb join together at the end of a subordinate clause (see also 10.6):

Wir waren sehr müde, als wir endlich **ankamen**.
We were very tired when we finally **arrived**.

Here, **ankamen** is a joined-together form of the simple past tense:

wir kamen endlich an ····⟩ … als wir endlich ankamen

NOTE that there must be a comma between the two clauses.

All the examples so far have shown subordinate clauses following main clauses. However, it is equally possible to have the subordinate clause first:

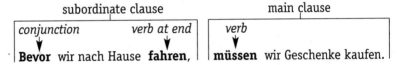

NOTE what happens to the main clause – it starts with its verb. Whenever the subordinate clause comes before the main clause, the sentence ends up having two verbs together in the middle. In writing, there is a comma between them.

This diagram is a summary of the word order used in sentences containing a subordinate clause:

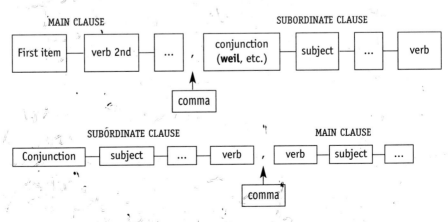

Finer points of subordinate clauses

a The subject of a subordinate clause should always come right at the beginning of it, after the conjunction:

Obwohl **die meisten Leute heutzutage** Fernsehen haben, war es nicht immer so.
Although **nowadays most people** have television, it was not always so.

b NOTE this surprising and unusual refinement of the usual 'verb last' rule for subordinate clauses. When there are **two infinitives** in the subordinate clause, the part of **haben** or **werden** which goes with the infinitives is placed *before* them:

Es tut mir leid, dass ich dir nicht **habe helfen können**.
I am sorry that I **have** not **been able to help** you.

Es ist klar, dass man mehr Straßen **wird bauen müssen**.
It is clear that they **will have to build** more roads.

9.9 Relative clauses – *Relativsätze*

What is a relative clause?

A relative clause is a particular type of subordinate clause. It is a clause inserted after a noun to give further information about that noun. Here are two English examples:

The man **who lives next door** is a policeman.
The coat **which/that I bought** yesterday was very expensive.

The relative clauses in these two sentences give further information about *the man* and *the coat*. In English, we usually introduce relative clauses with *who*, *which* or *that*. These words are called relative pronouns. In the second example above, the *which* or *that* could even have been left out altogether:

The coat **I bought yesterday** was very expensive.

German always requires the relative pronoun.

Relative pronouns

Singular				Plural for all three genders
	m.	**f.**	**neut.**	
nom.	der	die	das	die
acc.	den	die	das	die
gen.	dessen	deren	dessen	deren
dat.	dem	der	dem	denen

Notice that most of these forms are the same as those in the **der/die/das** marker tables (see 2.4). The ones which differ are the genitive forms and the dative plural.

How to choose the correct relative pronoun

The *gender* of the relative pronoun depends on the word you are referring back to:

Der Mann, der nebenan wohnt, ist Polizist.
The man who lives next door is a policeman.

Die Lampe, die auf dem Tisch steht, war sehr teuer.
The lamp that's standing on the table was very expensive.

Here we have **der** referring back to **der Mann** (m.), and **die** referring back to **die** Lampe (f.). Notice that the verbs in the relative clauses (here: **wohnt**, **steht**) are at the end of those clauses. This is because relative clauses are a type of subordinate clause. In the plural, there is no problem of gender, of course:

Die Schuhe, die im Schaufenster sind, sehen am schönsten aus.
The shoes that are in the shop window look the nicest.

NOTE that, in German, relative clauses must be enclosed by commas.

The *case* of the relative pronoun depends on *the part the relative pronoun is playing inside the relative clause*. In the three examples given so far, the relative pronouns were all nominative, because they were the subjects of their clauses. We can see this, if we look at the first one again:

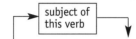

Der **Mann**, der nebenan **wohnt**, ist Polizist.

However, the relative pronoun can also be the direct object (accusative) of its clause:

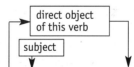

Der Mann, **den ich** gestern **besuchte**, ist Polizist.
The man **whom I visited yesterday** is a policeman.

The underlying idea of this relative clause is *I* (subject) *visited the man* (direct object).

The dative pronouns are needed for the indirect object of the relative clause, or after prepositions requiring the dative (see 3.6):

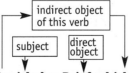

Die Frau, **der ich den Brief schickte**, wohnt in Kiel.
The woman **to whom I sent the letter** lives in Kiel. /
   The woman **I sent the letter to** lives in Kiel.

(Note that we cannot imitate this last English sentence in German!)

Der Junge, **mit dem** ich Tennis spiele, heißt Jürgen.
The boy **with whom I play tennis** is called Jürgen. /
   The boy **I play tennis with** is called Jürgen.

In the dative plural, **denen** is needed:

> Die Freunde, **mit denen** ich in Urlaub fahre, kommen aus der Schweiz.
> The friends **with whom I'm going on holiday** come from Switzerland. /
> The friends **I'm going on holiday with** come from Switzerland.

The genitive forms **dessen** and **deren** are the German equivalents of *whose*.
dessen refers back to a *masculine* or *neuter singular* word, and **deren** refers
back to a *feminine singular* word or *any plural* word.

> Die Frau, **deren Sohn krank ist**, ist unsere Nachbarin.
> The woman **whose son is ill** is our neighbour.

> Der Junge, **dessen Vater im Ausland arbeitet**, wohnt bei seiner Mutter.
> The boy **whose father works abroad** lives with his mother.

Remember to choose **dessen** or **deren** according to the word you are referring
back to, *not* according to the word that follows.

The 'extended participial phrase'

In formal written German, relative clauses are often replaced by a construction in which
the information is 'piled up' before the noun. This usually involves either a past or present
participle:

> **Der Plan, den der Minister vorschlug**, würde zwanzig Millionen kosten.
> ⤳ **Der vom Minister vorgeschlagene*** Plan würde zwanzig Millionen kosten.
> The plan that the minister proposed would cost twenty million.
> (Literally: 'The by the minister proposed plan ... ')

> **Die Sommerferien, die morgen beginnen**, werden sechs Wochen dauern.
> ⤳ **Die morgen beginnenden Sommerferien*** werden sechs Wochen dauern.
> The summer holidays that begin tomorrow will last six weeks.
> (Literally: 'The tomorrow beginning summer holidays ... ')

*Note that normal adjective endings are required (**der ... vorgeschlagene Plan,
die ... beginnenden Sommerferien** – see 2.4).

9.10   Relative clauses: *alles, was ... ,* etc.

When referring back to something less specific than a definite noun, **was** is
used to introduce the relative clause, instead of a form of **der/die/das**. This
often occurs after **alles**, **etwas**, **nichts** or a superlative such as **das Beste**.

> Ich mag **alles, was** gut schmeckt.
> I like **everything that** tastes good.

> **Nichts, was** Peter sagt, ist interessant.
> **Nothing that** Peter says is interesting.

> Das ist **das Beste**, was ich für dich tun kann.
> That's **the best** (thing) **that** I can do for you.

NOTE that **was**, when used in this way, introduces a subordinate clause with the
verb at the end. Note, too, that commas must be used.

9.11 Two-part conjunctions: *entweder ... oder ...* , etc.

a **entweder ... oder ...** means *either ... or ...*

> **Entweder** du machst deine Hausaufgaben, **oder** du bekommst kein Taschengeld.
> **Either** you do your homework, **or** you get no pocket-money.

NOTE that neither **entweder** nor **oder** affects word order.

b **weder ... noch ...** means *neither ... nor ...*

> **Weder** mein Bruder **noch** meine Schwester spielt Federball.
> **Neither** my brother **nor** my sister plays badminton.

c **sowohl ... als auch ...** means *both ... and ...*

> **Sowohl** meine Eltern **als auch** meine Lehrer wollen, dass ich Arzt werde.
> **Both** my parents **and** my teachers want me to become a doctor.

9.12 *nicht* and word order

nicht: *introduction*

nicht means *not* and is the most usual way of making a German sentence negative.

> Herr Braun arbeitet **nicht**.
> Herr Braun does **not** work.

NOTE that English often includes the verb *do* in negative sentences. This does not happen in German.

The German equivalent of *not a*, *no* and *not any* is not **nicht** but **kein** (see also 2.7).

> Das ist **kein** Problem.
> That is **not** a problem / **no** problem.

> Ich habe **kein** Geld.
> I have **no** money. / I haven't **any** money.

> Ich habe **keine** Briefmarken.
> I have **no** stamps. / I haven't **any** stamps.

Where to place *nicht* in the sentence

As you become more and more familiar with German, you will gradually get a 'feel' for the correct position of **nicht** in the sentence. The following rules are not the whole story, but will be of some help.

Rule 1: when there is any subject or object after the verb, **nicht** is usually left until the end (or as near as possible to the end) of the sentence.

> Ich sah den Film **nicht**.
> I did not see the film.

Ich habe den Film **nicht** gesehen.
I did not see the film.

Den Film habe ich **nicht** gesehen.
I did not see the film.

Schmeckt dir das Brot **nicht**?
Don't you like the bread?

Rule 2: when the items following the verb are not subjects or objects, **nicht** usually follows the verb − i.e. the verb is second in the sentence and **nicht** is third.

Ich bin **nicht** krank.
I am not ill.

Ich gehe **nicht** in die Stadt.
I'm not going to town.

Rule 3: when the 'time−manner−place' rule is involved (see 9.5), **nicht** usually comes before the expression of manner (if there is one) or else before the expression of place.

Ich gehe heute **nicht** zu Fuß zur Schule.
I'm not going to school on foot today.

Ich gehe heute **nicht** zur Schule.
I'm not going to school today.

Rule 4: when you want to say '*not **this**, but **this***' in German, **nicht** comes before the thing that is being ruled out.

Ich spiele **nicht** Tennis sondern Federball.
I'm playing not tennis but badminton.

10 Verbs

10.1 What is a verb?

Verbs are words which usually denote an activity (e.g. *go*, *work*, *buy*), and so verbs are often labelled as 'action' words. However, some of the most frequently used verbs denote 'in-action' (e.g. *be*, *have*, *remain*, *stand*). No activity is going on at all: these verbs describe a static situation – a state of affairs. So, while it is convenient to think of verbs as actions, always remember that there is this other small but highly important group.

Verbs have a form called the infinitive – this is the form listed in a dictionary or vocabulary. In English the infinitive is introduced by *to*. In German the infinitive is just one word, ending with **-en** or **-n**:

spiel**en**	*to play*
arbeit**en**	*to work*
angel**n**	*to fish*

Removing this **-en** or **-n** reveals the stem of the verb. To this stem, the various verb endings are added. We have some verb endings in English; for example, from the verb *work*, we have *he work**s*** and *I work**ed***. German has more verb endings than English, however. These verb forms are explained in the following sections.

10.2 The present tense – *das Präsens*

The present tense describes what is happening now, or what usually happens. The German present tense corresponds to a variety of English verb forms. For example, **ich schwimme** can be translated into English as:

I swim
I am swimming
I do swim

 Be careful not to use German verb forms such as ~~ich bin schwimmen~~ or ~~ich tue schwimmen~~. *I am swimming* and *I do swim* are both simply: **ich schwimme**.

10.3 The present: regular weak verbs (*regelmäßige schwache Verben*)

Regular weak verbs are verbs without any peculiarities, which all have the same endings as each other. There are thousands of these verbs. We shall take as an example the verb **spielen** (*to play*):

ich spiel**e**	*I play, I am playing, I do play*
du spiel**st**	*you play, you are playing, you do play*
er spiel**t**	*he/it plays, etc.*
sie spiel**t**	*she/it plays, etc.*
es spiel**t**	*it plays, etc.*
wir spiel**en**	*we play, etc.*
ihr spiel**t**	*you play, etc.*
Sie spiel**en**	*you play, etc.*
sie spiel**en**	*they play, etc.*

The pronouns (**ich**, **du**, **er**, etc.) used here are explained in 4.2–4.4. In all verbs, in all tenses, the pronouns **er**, **sie** and **es** share a common verb form (here, all three share the form **spielt**). This is also the form used with a singular noun subject (e.g. **Meine Schwester spiel*t* Tennis**) and with **man** (meaning *one* – see 4.2).

In all verbs, in all tenses, the pronouns **Sie** (*you*) and **sie** (*they*) share a common verb form (here, both share the form **spiel*en***). This is also the form used with a plural noun subject (e.g. **Meine Freunde spiel*en* Tennis**). The same verb form is also always used for **wir** (*we*).

10.4   Verbs with a slightly irregular present tense

10.4a   Verbs like *arbeiten*

These are verbs in which it would be difficult to pronounce the endings **-t** and **-st** when added to the stem.

For example, **arbeiten** has the stem **arbeit-**, so **-t** cannot be added directly. To solve this problem, **-e-** is inserted before **-st** and **-t** endings:

ich	arbeit**e**	wir	arbeit**en**
du	arbeit**est**	ihr	arbeit**et**
er/sie/es	arbeit**et**	Sie/sie	arbeit**en**

Other common verbs like **arbeiten** include:

abtrocknen*	*to dry*
antworten	*to answer*
baden	*to have a bath / to bathe*
heiraten	*to get married*
kosten	*to cost*
reden	*to speak*
regnen	*to rain*
retten	*to rescue*
warten	*to wait*
zeichnen	*to draw*

*Separable prefixes (see 10.6) are shown in **bold type**.

10.4b Verbs like *angeln*

These are verbs which have the ending **-n** where most verbs have **-en**:

ich	ang(e)le	wir	angel**n**
du	angelst	ihr	angelt
er/sie/es	angelt	Sie/sie	angel**n**

Other common verbs like **angeln** include:

bummeln	*to stroll*
rudern	*to row*
sammeln	*to collect*
segeln	*to sail*
wandern	*to hike*

10.4c Verbs in which the stem ends in an *s* sound

These verbs drop the **-s-** from the **-st** ending in the **du** part of the verb:

du **heißt**	*you are called*	from **heißen**
du **niest**	*you sneeze*	from **niesen**

10.5 The present: strong verbs (*starke Verben*)

Strong verbs are verbs which make alterations to their stem as well as adding the normal endings. As an example, here is the verb **sprechen** (*to speak*):

ich	spreche	wir	sprechen
du	sprichst	ihr	sprecht [💣 No change here.]
er/sie/es	spricht	Sie/sie	sprechen

sprechen changes **e** to **i** in the **du** and **er/sie/es** parts. Other strong verbs make a variety of different changes, but the parts of the verb which are affected are always the same: **du** and **er/sie/es**.

Other examples in brief form:

fahren:	du f**ä**hrst, er/sie/es f**ä**hrt	*to go, to drive*
sehen:	du s**ie**hst, er/sie/es s**ie**ht	*to see*
nehmen:	du n**imm**st, er/sie/es n**imm**t	*to take*
laufen:	du l**äu**fst, er/sie/es l**äu**ft	*to run, to walk*

There are many strong verbs. You can find them in the verb list (10.43).

Strong verbs with slight peculiarities

These verbs have shortened the normal endings:

lesen:	du **liest**, er/sie/es liest	*to read*
essen*:	du **isst**, er/sie/es isst	*to eat*
halten:	du hältst, er/sie/es **hält**	*to hold, to stop*
treten:	du trittst, er/sie/es **tritt**	*to step, to kick*
einladen:	du lädst ein, er/sie/es **lädt** ein	*to invite*

*****fressen** and **vergessen** are similar.

For more on strong verbs, see 10.14 and 10.21.

10.6 Separable verbs (*trennbare Verben*) – all tenses

These are verbs which consist of two parts: a basic verb, plus a prefix. We have something like this in English:

> I **switched** the light **off**.
> I often **go out** in the evenings.

In English, the two parts of the verb are always separated. In German, they are sometimes separated and sometimes together. Here are some examples based on the separable verb *auf***machen** (*to open*):

> Ich kann die Tür nicht **aufmachen**.   ⟵ *infinitive*: joined together
> I can't open the door.
>
> Ich **mache** die Tür **auf**.   ⟵ *present tense*: separated
> I am opening the door.
>
> Ich **machte** die Tür **auf**.   ⟵ *simple past tense*: separated
> I opened the door.   (see 10.13)
>
> Ich **habe** die Tür **aufgemacht**.   ⟵ *perfect tense*: joined together
> I opened the door.   (see 10.17)
>
> Vati weiß, dass ich die Tür **aufmache**.⟵ *subordinate clause*: joined
> Dad knows that I'm opening the door.   together (see 9.8)

10.6a How to use *hin* and *her*

These two words usually form themselves into separable verb prefixes, such as **hin**gehen, **her**kommen, etc.

The basic idea behind **hin** is going away, and the basic idea behind **her** is coming towards.

Used on their own, **hin** is short for **dorthin** and means (*to*) *there* and **her** is short for **hierher** and means (*to*) *here*.

Here are some examples of **hin** and **her** used as words on their own:

> Morgen gehen wir **hin**.
> Tomorrow we'll go **there**.
>
> Komm **her**!
> Come **here**!
>
> Du sollst **her**kommen!
> You're to come **here**!
>
> Wollen wir **hin**gehen?
> Shall we go **there**?

hin can also mean *down*, as in the verbs *hin***legen** and *hin***stellen** (*to put something down*).

Very often, **hin** and **her** are combined into longer prefixes, such as:

hinein-/herein-	*in*
hinaus-/heraus-	*out*
hinauf-/herauf-	*up*
hinunter-/herunter-	*down*
hinab-/herab-	*down*

Here are some examples of these in use:

Komm **herein**!
Come **in**!

Wir gingen zur Burg **hinauf**.
We went **up** to the castle.

Wollen wir **hinein**gehen?
Shall we go **in**?

Wir gingen ins Tal **hinab/hinunter**.
We went **down** into the valley.

These prefixes are often used to strengthen what has, in fact, already been said:

Ich ging in die Stadt **hinein**.
I went into the town.

Er kam aus dem Haus **heraus**.
He came out of the house.

To say *up the hill* or *down the street*, the relevant noun is put into the accusative:

Ich ging **den Berg hinauf**.
I went **up the mountain**.

Ich ging **die Straße hinunter/hinab**.
I went **down the street/road**.

In conversation (especially in northern Germany), the **hin-** forms of these prefixes are not much used. The **her-** forms are used instead, often with the **her-** shortened to simply '**r-**:

Ich ging in die Stadt '**rein**.
I went into the town.

Ich ging die Straße '**runter**.
I went down the street/road.

10.7 The present: reflexive verbs (*reflexive Verben*)

These are verbs in which the subject and direct object are the same person or thing – i.e. the subject does something to himself/herself/itself. Here, as an example, is the present tense of **sich wiegen** (*to weigh oneself*):

ich	wiege **mich**	wir	wiegen **uns**
du	wiegst **dich**	ihr	wiegt **euch**
er/sie/es	wiegt **sich**	Sie/sie	wiegen **sich**

Ich wiege mich means *I weigh myself*, **du wiegst dich** means *you weigh yourself*, etc. The words **mich**, **dich**, **sich**, etc. are known as *reflexive pronouns*.

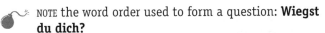 NOTE the word order used to form a question: **Wiegst du dich?**

10.7a Common reflexive verbs

There are quite a few of these in German. Many of them are verbs whose English equivalents do not involve *myself, yourself*, etc. Here is a useful selection (separable prefixes are shown in bold type):

sich **ab**trocknen	*to dry oneself*
sich **an**ziehen	*to get dressed*
sich ärgern	*to get annoyed*
sich ausruhen	*to have a rest*
sich ausziehen	*to get undressed*
sich beeilen	*to hurry up*
sich entschuldigen	*to apologise*
sich erinnern an + acc.	*to remember*
sich erkälten	*to catch a cold*
sich freuen	*to be pleased*
sich **hin**legen	*to lie down*
sich **hin**setzen	*to sit down*
sich kämmen	*to comb one's hair*
sich rasieren	*to have a shave*
sich schminken	*to put make-up on*
sich treffen (see 12.3)	*to meet (each other)*
sich **um**ziehen	*to get changed*
sich waschen	*to have a wash*

For the perfect tense of reflexive verbs, see 10.25.

10.7b Expressions with the reflexive pronoun in the dative

When a person does something for his or her own benefit, German often uses the formula: verb + dative reflexive pronoun + a direct object (acc.). Many of these verbs are connected with the idea of *looking after oneself*. A typical example is **sich die Hände waschen** (*to wash one's hands*):

ich	wasche	**mir**	die Hände
du	wäschst	**dir**	die Hände
er/sie/es	wäscht	**sich**	die Hände
wir	waschen	**uns**	die Hände
ihr	wascht	**euch**	die Hände
Sie/sie	waschen	**sich**	die Hände

Notice these dative reflexive pronouns. Most of them are the same as the ordinary accusative reflexive pronouns shown earlier in this section, but **mich** has become **mir**, and **dich** has become **dir**.

Here are some examples of the same expression in other contexts and tenses:

Ich muss mir die Hände waschen.
I must wash my hands.

Dann wusch ich mir die Hände.
Then I washed my hands.

Ich habe mir die Hände gewaschen.
I washed my hands.

Other similar expressions are:

sich die Zähne/Schuhe putzen	*to clean one's teeth/shoes*
sich etwas **an**sehen	*to have a look at something*
sich etwas kaufen	*to buy oneself something*
sich etwas **aus**suchen	*to find oneself something*

10.7c To have something done for oneself – using *lassen*

To say that you have/get something done for yourself (e.g. *have your hair cut*), use **lassen** with an infinitive (see also 10.32a). This often involves a dative reflexive pronoun, as in these examples:

Ich lasse mir die Haare **schneiden**.
I am having my hair cut.

Schmidts **lassen** sich ein Haus **bauen**.
The Schmidts are having (themselves) a house built.

For the perfect tense of **lassen** + *infinitive,* see 10.27.

10.8 The present: modal verbs (*Modalverben*)

These are six verbs which are very commonly used in German. They are irregular, and their present tenses are therefore set out in full below. They are mostly used with another verb, which is always in the infinitive form and at the end (or as near as possible to the end) of the clause or sentence. A few examples only are given here. Many more can be found in Chapter 12.

können *can, to be able to*

ich	kann [no **e** ending]		wir	können
du	kannst		ihr	könnt
er/sie/es	kann [no **t** ending]		Sie/sie	können

Was **kann** ich für dich **tun**?
What **can I do** for you?

Leider **können** wir nicht zur Party **mitkommen**.
Unfortunately we **can't come** to the party.

NOTE that the infinitives **tun** and **mitkommen** come at the end of these examples. For other examples, see 12.2.

müssen *must, to have to*

ich	muss [no **e** ending]		wir	müssen
du	musst		ihr	müsst
er/sie/es	muss [no **t** ending]		Sie/sie	müssen

Du **musst** deine Hausaufgaben **machen**.
You **must do** your homework.

 NOTE: **müssen** + **nicht** = *don't have to.*

Du **musst nicht** in die Disko **gehen**.
You **don't have to go** to the disco.

This does *not* mean *You **mustn't** go to the disco,* which is expressed using **dürfen** (see below).

wollen   *to want to*

ich	will [no **e** ending]	wir	wollen
du	willst	ihr	wollt
er/sie/es	will [no **t** ending]	Sie/sie	wollen

This verb means *want to*. It is *not* the equivalent of *will* in English and is *not* used to form the future tense! (For the future, see 10.29.)

Susanne **will** ein neues Kleid **kaufen**.
Susanne **wants to buy** a new dress.

NOTE that **wollen wir** ...? is used for *shall we* ...?

Wollen wir ein Eis **kaufen**?
Shall we buy an ice-cream?

(See also 10.41b)

sollen   *to be supposed to, to be meant to, to be due to*

ich	soll [no **e** ending]	wir	sollen
du	sollst	ihr	sollt
er/sie/es	soll [no **t** ending]	Sie/sie	sollen

This verb has many English equivalents. Often we say *shall* (as in: *What shall I do?* meaning *What am I supposed to do?*), but **sollen** has nothing to do with the future tense and is not used for *shall* in sentences such as *I shall go to London tomorrow.* (For the future, see 10.29.) Basically, **sollen** has a meaning which is a weaker version of **müssen**. **müssen** says what *must be done*, **sollen** says what *is supposed to be done*. (The separable prefix is shown in **bold italics** – see 10.6.)

Wann **soll** ich *zurück***sein**?
When **shall I be back**? / When **am I supposed to be back**?

Soll ich dir **helfen**?
Shall I help you?

Er **soll** krank **sein**.
He's **supposed to be** ill.

There is also a special form of **sollen**, which means *ought to* or *should*. This is **sollte**. Here is an example:

Du bist doch krank. Du **solltest** zum Arzt **gehen**.
You're ill. You **ought to** / **should go to** the doctor's.

dürfen   *may, to be allowed to*

ich	darf [no **e** ending]	wir	dürfen
du	darfst	ihr	dürft
er/sie/es	darf [no **t** ending]	Sie/sie	dürfen

This verb is about having *permission* to do things:

Ich **darf** nicht **schwimmen gehen.**
I'm not **allowed to go swimming.**

In der Schule **darf** man nicht **essen.**
You're not **allowed to eat** in school.

When asking for permission, **darf ich?** is more polite than **kann ich?**:

Darf ich ins Kino **gehen**?
May I go to the cinema?

Kann ich ins Kino **gehen**?
Can I go to the cinema?

dürfen + **nicht** is often the equivalent of English *must not*:

Das **darfst** du **nicht machen.**
You **mustn't do** that. [= You're not allowed to do that.]

 REMEMBER that **müssen** + **nicht** means *don't have to*, not *mustn't* (see above).

mögen   *to like*

ich	mag [no **e** ending]	wir	mögen
du	magst	ihr	mögt
er/sie/es	mag [no **t** ending]	Sie/sie	mögen

This verb is different from the other modals, since it is mostly used without another verb in the infinitive. It means *like*, and is especially used for liking *foods* and *people*:

Ich **mag** ihn (gern).
I **like** him.

Ich **mag** ihn **nicht.**
I **don't like** him.

Tomaten **mag** ich **sehr gern.**
I **really like** tomatoes.

Bananen **mag** ich **nicht so gern.**
I'm **not keen on** bananas.

Ich **mag keine** Apfelsinen.
I **don't like** oranges.

The most common form of **mögen** is not the present tense, but **möchte** (*would like*):

Ich möchte bitte ein Kilo Birnen.
I'd like a kilo of pears, please.

NOTE that **möchte** has a present tense meaning. For other tenses, use parts of the verb **wollen**:

Ich wollte ein Kilo Birnen.
I **wanted** a kilo of pears.

Leaving out the second verb after a modal verb

This is never compulsory, but it is often done in spoken German. In these examples, the verb in brackets could easily be left out because the verb intended is obvious:

Ich **muss** zum Arzt (**gehen**).
I **must go** to the doctor's.

Ich **will** nach Berlin (**fahren**).
I **want to go** to Berlin.

Udo **kann** sehr gut Englisch (**sprechen**).
Udo **can speak** English very well.

Ich **kann** nicht **mit**(**kommen**).
I **can't come** with you.

gehen and **fahren** are the verbs most often left out.

(Other tenses of modal verbs are described in 10.15 and 10.27.)

10.9 The present: *sein, haben, werden, wissen*

Apart from the modals, there are four verbs which have an irregular present tense:

sein	*to be*
haben	*to have*
werden	*to become*
wissen	*to know*

sein *to be*

ich	**bin**	wir	**sind**
du	**bist**	ihr	**seid**
er/sie/es	**ist**	Sie/sie	**sind**

This verb is also irregular in English: *I am, you are, he is*, etc.

Here is an example of **sein** in use:

Wie alt **bist du**, Robert?   **Ich bin** sechzehn Jahre alt.
How old **are you**, Robert? **I am** sixteen years old.

sein is also used to help form the perfect tense of some verbs (see 10.22).

> NOTE that, between two nouns, **sein** is used in the plural if either of the two nouns is plural:
>
> Das größte Problem **sind** Verkehrsunfälle.
> The biggest problem **is** road accidents.

haben   *to have*

ich	**habe**	wir	**haben**
du	**hast**	ihr	**habt**
er/sie/es	**hat**	Sie/sie	**haben**

Hast du Geschwister? Ja, **ich habe** zwei Schwestern.
Have you any brothers or sisters? Yes, **I have** two sisters.

haben is also used to help form the perfect tense of most verbs (see 10.17 onwards).

In some expressions, German has **haben** where English has the verb *to be*:

Ich habe Hunger/Durst.
I am hungry/thirsty.

Ich habe recht/unrecht.
I am right/wrong

werden   *to become*

ich	**werde**	wir	**werden**
du	**wirst**	ihr	**werdet**
er/sie/es	**wird**	Sie/sie	**werden**

In English, we use a number of different verbs to convey the meaning *become*. These are all expressed by **werden** in German:

Ich **werde** müde.
I'm **becoming/getting/growing** tired.

werden is also used to help form the future tense (see 10.29) and the passive (see 10.34).

wissen   *to know*

ich	**weiß** [no **e** ending]	wir	**wissen**
du	**weißt**	ihr	**wisst**
er/sie/es	**weiß** [no **t** ending]	Sie/sie	**wissen**

Weißt du, wo der Bahnhof ist?   Nein, **das weiß ich nicht.**
Do you know where the station is?   No, **I don't know (that).**

In conversation, **das weiß ich nicht** is often shortened to **weiß ich nicht**.

This verb is used to mean *to know* in the sense of knowing information. It is *not* used to mean *to know* in the sense of *to be acquainted with* (which is **kennen**). For more on this, see 10.42.

10.10 Commands, instructions and suggestions

We use command forms to get people to do things (see also 12.3). Command forms are not necessarily used for ordering people about. They can be polite requests. For example, **entschuldigen Sie, bitte** (*excuse me, please*) is a command form, but it is also polite. In German, command forms vary depending on the person you are talking to. These are described below. The difference between **du**, **ihr** and **Sie** is treated in 4.3.

10.10a Commands to use when talking to someone you address as *du*

Basic rule: take the **du** part of the present tense, and remove the word **du** and the **-st** ending:

du spielst	⋯⋯⟩	**spiel!**	*play!*	(from the verb **spielen**)
du gibst	⋯⋯⟩	**gib!**	*give!*	(from the verb **geben**)
du sprichst	⋯⋯⟩	**sprich!**	*speak!*	(from the verb **sprechen**)

This means that strong verbs (such as **sprechen** – see 10.5) keep the change made in their stem in the **du** part.

EXCEPTION: with strong verbs in which Umlaut is added in the **du** part, this is dropped in the command:

du fährst	⋯⋯⟩	**fahr!**	*go!*	(from the verb **fahren**)
du schläfst	⋯⋯⟩	**schlaf!**	*sleep!*	(from the verb **schlafen**)
du läufst	⋯⋯⟩	**lauf!**	*run!*	(from the verb **laufen**)

NOTE: **du isst** ⋯⋯⟩ **iss!** (*eat!*); and **du liest** ⋯⋯⟩ **lies!** (*read!*).

Sometimes, **du** commands are given the ending **-e**. This is usually optional, and in spoken German the **-e** is mostly left off. Here are some command forms showing the **-e** ending:

singe!	OR sing!	*sing!*
schwimme!	OR schwimm!	*swim!*

However, some strong verbs cannot have the **-e** ending:

iss!	*eat!*
nimm!	*take!*

So it is usually safest to leave off the **-e** ending. Two small groups of verbs must have the **-e** ending, however. These are the verbs such as **arbeiten** and **angeln** (see 10.4). The only correct forms here are:

arbeite!	*work!*
ang(e)le!	*fish!*

entschuldigen (*to excuse*) has the form **entschuldige!** (*excuse me!*)

sein (*to be*) has an irregular command form: **sei!**

Sei still!   *Be quiet!*

10.10b Commands to use when talking to people you address as *ihr*

Rule: take the **ihr** part of the present tense and remove the word **ihr**:

ihr schwimmt	⋯⋯⟩	**schwimmt!**	*swim!*
ihr schlaft	⋯⋯⟩	**schlaft!**	*sleep!*
ihr lauft	⋯⋯⟩	**lauft!**	*run!*
ihr arbeitet	⋯⋯⟩	**arbeitet!**	*work!*
ihr seid	⋯⋯⟩	**seid** (still)**!**	*be (quiet)!*

10.10c Commands to use when talking to people you address as *Sie*

Rule: take the **Sie** part of the present tense and turn the words around.

Sie schwimmen ·····⟩ **schwimmen Sie!** *swim!*
Sie schlafen ·····⟩ **schlafen Sie!** *sleep!*

For **sein** (*to be*), the form is **seien Sie!**

Seien Sie still!   *Be quiet!*

10.10d 'To whom it may concern!' – commands and instructions

In this kind of an instruction – to anyone it may concern – the infinitive is used. Instructions like these are especially common in written German, in recipes, in instructions, and in public notices and signs.

Aufmachen!
Open up! [i.e. open the door]

Nicht **schießen!**
No shooting!

Bitte sofort **anrufen.**
Please telephone at once.

Die Schnitzel **klopfen**, **salzen** und **pfeffern.**
Beat the schnitzels to flatten them out, then season with salt and pepper.

10.10e *Let's ...* (suggestion)

wir tanzen ·····⟩ **tanzen wir!** *let's dance*
wir fangen an ·····⟩ **fangen wir an!** *let's start*

For **sein**, the form is **seien wir**:

Seien wir vorsichtig!   *Let's be careful!*

See also 12.3.

> NOTE that there are two other ways of expressing *let's* in German:
>
> Wir wollen tanzen! *Let's dance!*
> Lasst uns gehen! *Let's go!*

10.11 The present participle: German and English compared

In German this verb form is made by adding **-d** to the infinitive. German present participles are mainly used as adjectives, with adjective endings. The corresponding English word usually ends in *-ing*.

aufregen   to excite ·····⟩ **aufregend**

Das war ein **aufregender** Film.
That was an **exciting** film.

lächeln   to smile ·····⟩ **lächelnd**

sein **lächelndes** Gesicht
his **smiling** face

And, like adjectives, present participles can also be used as adverbs:

,,Guten Tag'', sagte sie **lächelnd**.
'Hello', she said, **smiling(ly)**.

Despite these examples, English forms ending in *-ing* cannot usually be translated by German present participles. In sentences such as the following one, a clause is usually needed instead:

Arriving at the station, I bought a ticket.
Als ich am Bahnhof ankam, kaufte ich eine Fahrkarte.
(= When I arrived at the station, I bought a ticket.)

In other contexts, other solutions may be needed:

We enjoyed **playing football**.
Es hat uns Spaß gemacht, **Fußball zu spielen**.
(= It was fun for us to play football.)

10.12 The simple past tense – *das Präteritum*

You need this tense to talk about the past. It is called 'simple' because the verb consists of just one word. The simple past also has other other names. Some people call it the *imperfect,* others the *preterite*. In German, it is usually called **das Präteritum** or **das Imperfekt**.

The simple past corresponds to a variety of English past tenses. For example, **ich spielte** can be translated into English as: *I played, I used to play, I was playing* or *I did play*.

Be careful not to invent German past tense forms such as ~~ich war spielen~~. This is not the German past tense! *I was playing* is simply **ich spielte**.

10.13 The simple past: regular and slightly irregular weak verbs

There are thousands of verbs which follow the pattern of **spielen**:

spielen | *to play*

ich	spiel**te**	wir	spiel**ten**
du	spiel**test**	ihr	spiel**tet**
er/sie/es	spiel**te** [no **t** ending]	Sie/sie	spiel**ten**

Examples of this tense in action:

Gestern **spielte ich** Federball.
Yesterday **I played** badminton.

Als Kind **spielte ich** Fußball.
As a child, **I played / used to play** football.

Ich spielte Karten, als sie kam.
I was playing cards when she came.

<u>Verbs with a slightly irregular simple past</u>
Verbs such as **arbeiten** (see 10.4) have an **-e-** before the **-te** endings:

ich arbeit**e**te, du arbeit**e**test, er arbeit**e**te, etc.

10.14   The simple past: strong verbs (*starke Verben*)

We have strong verbs in the English simple past tense – verbs which alter their stem rather than add the past tense ending **-ed**:

I sing ····} I sang,   write ····} I wrote,   I drive ····} I drove

The German strong verbs behave in a similar way: they change their stem in the simple past. The endings they use are as shown in the example verb:

singen   *to sing*

ich	sang [no **e** ending]	wir	sang**en**
du	sang**st**	ihr	sang**t**
er/sie/es	sang [no **t** ending]	Sie/sie	sang**en**

There are many other strong verbs besides **singen**. They can be found in the verb list (10.43).

10.15   The simple past: modal verbs (*Modalverben*)

In the simple past, the six modal verbs (see 10.8) have the **-te** endings of regular weak verbs (as in 10.13), but some of them make a slight alteration to their stem as well:

können	····}	ich **konnte**	*I could, was able to*
müssen	····}	ich **musste**	*I had to*
wollen	····}	ich **wollte**	*I wanted to*
sollen	····}	ich **sollte**	*I was to, was supposed to*
dürfen	····}	ich **durfte**	*I was allowed to*
mögen	····}	ich **mochte**	*I liked*

NOTE that the modals which have Umlaut in the infinitive all lose the Umlaut in the simple past. Here are examples of three of them in use:

Leider **konnte** ich gestern nicht kommen.
Unfortunately I **couldn't / was not able to** come yesterday.

Ich **musste** nach London fahren.
I **had to** go to London.

Ich **sollte** zur Bank gehen.
I **was supposed** to go to the bank.

10.16   The simple past: irregular verbs

There are a few verbs with an irregular simple past, and they are shown here. Most of them combine a change in their stem with the **-te** endings of weak verbs. Because of this, they are often known as *mixed* verbs.

haben	*to have*	····}	ich **hatte**
kennen*	*to know*	····}	ich **kannte**
wissen*	*to know*	····}	ich **wusste**
bringen	*to bring*	····}	ich **brachte**
verbringen	*to spend (time)*	····}	ich **verbrachte**
denken	*to think*	····}	ich **dachte**
rennen	*to run*	····}	ich **rannte**

nennen	*to name*		ich **nannte**
brennen	*to burn*	⟶	ich **brannte**
verbrennen	*to burn (something)*	⟶	ich **verbrannte**

*For the difference between **kennen** and **wissen**, see 10.42.

The most irregular is **werden** (*to become*). It has endings in **-de** instead of **-te**:

ich	**wurde**	wir	**wurden**
du	**wurdest**	ihr	**wurdet**
er/sie/es	**wurde**	Sie/sie	**wurden**

 sein (*to be*) is *not* irregular in the simple past. It acts as a strong verb, and has the simple past ich **war**, du **warst**, er/sie/es **war**, etc.

10.17 The perfect tense – *das Perfekt*

Apart from the simple past tense (described in the last five sections above), German has another major past tense. This is the perfect. It is made up of two elements: the present tense of either **haben** or **sein** (see 10.22) *plus* a special verb form called the *past participle*. For example:

Ich **habe** Tischtennis **gespielt**.

present tense of **haben**	past participle of **spielen**

I **played** table-tennis.

Ich **bin** mit dem Auto **gefahren**.

present tense of **sein**	past participle of **fahren**

I **went** by car.

NOTE that the past participle is placed at the end of the clause.

Like other German tenses, the perfect corresponds to a variety of English tenses. For example, **ich habe gespielt** can be translated as *I played*, *I have played*, *I used to play* or *I did play*.

10.18 The perfect and the simple past compared

There is for practical purposes no real difference between the simple past and the perfect, although there are variations in usage. If you compare the English translations given for **ich spielte** in 10.12 and for **ich habe gespielt** in 10.17 above, you will see that they are largely identical.

In spoken German, both tenses are used, but there is a tendency to prefer the perfect. In South Germany, Switzerland and Austria, the simple past is very little used in speech – the perfect is used instead. As an English-speaking learner of German, you can use either tense when speaking about the past. You can treat the two tenses as interchangeable.

In written German, the simple past is the main tense to use. When writing a past tense story, you *must* use the simple past. In letter-writing, both tenses are equally acceptable.

10.19 The perfect: regular and slightly irregular weak verbs that take *haben*

The tense is constructed by using the present tense of **haben** (see 10.9) plus a past participle. This is made by taking the stem of the verb and putting **ge-** as a prefix before it and **-t** on the end of it.

spielen	to play	·····⟩	**ge**spiel**t**
tanzen	to dance	·····⟩	**ge**tanz**t**
zahlen	to pay	·····⟩	**ge**zahl**t**

The past participle is placed at the end (or as near as possible to the end) of the clause or sentence:

Gestern **habe ich** Tennis **gespielt**.
Yesterday **I played** tennis.

Dann **haben wir** in der Disko **getanzt**.
Then **we danced** at the disco.

Wir haben zehn Mark **gezahlt**.
We paid ten Marks.

In subordinate clauses (see 9.8), the word order is like this:

Heute bin ich müde, weil **ich** Tennis **gespielt habe**.
Today I am tired, because **I played** tennis.

Verbs with a slightly irregular past participle

Verbs such as **arbeiten** (see 10.4) have **-et** instead of **-t** on the end of the past participle:

Ich habe im Garten gearbeit**et**.
I worked in the garden.

10.20 The perfect: verbs with an inseparable prefix

Some verbs have an inseparable prefix (i.e. a prefix which never separates from the verb). They make their past participles without adding **ge-**. For example:

besuchen *to visit* ·····⟩ Ich habe meinen Onkel **besucht**.
I visited my uncle.

past participles without **ge-**

verkaufen *to sell* ·····⟩ Ich habe mein Fahrrad **verkauft**.
I sold my bike.

Inseparable prefixes include **er-**, **ent-**, **emp-**, **ge-**, **miss-** and **zer-**. Some typical inseparable verbs are:

erzählen	*to tell*
entschuldigen	*to excuse*
empfehlen	*to recommend*
gefallen	*to please*
missverstehen	*to misunderstand*
zerbrechen	*to smash*

NOTE that the last four of these are strong verbs (see 10.21).

10.21 The perfect: strong verbs (*starke Verben*)

The past participles of strong verbs can be found in the verb list (10.43). They start with **ge-** (or with one of the inseparable prefixes given in 10.20), but they almost all end in **-en**, instead of the **-t** used with weak verbs. Here are a few examples:

schreiben   *to write*   ····⟩   Ich habe einen Brief **ge**schrieb**en**.
I wrote a letter.

trinken   *to drink*   ····⟩   Wir haben Bier **ge**trunk**en**.
We drank beer.

beginnen   *to begin*   ····⟩   Der Film hat gerade **be**gonn**en**.
The film has just begun.

For more on strong verbs, see 10.5 and 10.14.

10.22 The perfect: with *haben* or *sein*?

Although the great majority of verbs form the perfect tense with **haben**, some take **sein** instead. The verbs concerned may be weak, strong, inseparable, separable, or any other type! So how do you tell which verbs take **sein**?

Rule 1: All verbs which have, or usually have, a direct object must take **haben**. These are traditionally known as *transitive* verbs. An example is **trinken**. You normally drink *something* (a direct object), so **trinken** takes **haben: ich habe Apfelsaft getrunken.**

Rule 2: Verbs without a direct object (*intransitive* verbs) also take **haben**, except for:

* Verbs denoting motion from place to place. These take **sein**. For example:

gehen   ····⟩   Ich **bin** zu Fuß **gegangen**.
····⟩   I went on foot.

fahren   ····⟩   Ulli **ist** nach Ulm **gefahren**.
····⟩   Ulli went to Ulm.

fliegen   ····⟩   Ich **bin** nach Amerika **geflogen**.
····⟩   I flew to America.

* Verbs denoting a change of state. These also take **sein**. For example:

aufwachen ····⟩   Ich **bin** früh **aufgewacht**.
····⟩   I woke up early.

sterben   ····⟩   Mein Hund **ist** 1983 **gestorben**.
····⟩   My dog died in 1983.

werden   ····⟩   Helga **ist** reich **geworden**.
····⟩   Helga became/got rich.

* Some other verbs. These two are the most important:

sein   ····⟩   Ich **bin** in Urlaub **gewesen**.
I was on holiday.

bleiben   ····⟩   Karin **ist** zu Hause **geblieben**.
Karin stayed at home.

Verbs which can take *haben* or *sein*

- Verbs denoting motion, such as **schwimmen** (*to swim*), **segeln** (*to sail*) and **rudern** (*to row*), sometimes take **haben** when they show motion *within one place* (i.e. not motion *from place to place*):

  Ich **habe** im Fluss **geschwommen**.
  I swam in the river.

  But **sein** is never wrong with these verbs. We can also say:

  Ich **bin** im Fluss **geschwommen**.
  I swam in the river.

  For English-speaking learners of German, it is safer to stick to **sein** with these verbs.

- Some verbs which have two different meanings need **sein** for one meaning and **haben** for the other. The main example of this that you are likely to meet is **fahren**. It normally means *to go* and takes **sein**:

  Gestern **sind** wir nach Wien **gefahren**.
  Yesterday we **went** to Vienna.

  However, **fahren** can also mean *to drive*, as in *to drive someone to a place*. In this meaning, it has a direct object. Under Rule 1 as above, verbs with a direct object must take **haben**:

  Meine Mutter **hat mich** zum Bahnhof **gefahren**.
  My mother **drove me** to the station.

  There are rare exceptions to some of the rules in this section, but the rules given here will cover virtually all the verbs you are likely to need.

10.23 The perfect: verbs ending in *-ieren*

These verbs are weak verbs, but they do *not* have the prefix **ge-** in their past participles:

telefonieren ⸱⸱⸱⸱⸱⸳ Ich **habe** mit Hans **telefoniert**.
I spoke to Hans on the phone.

reparieren ⸱⸱⸱⸱⸱⸳ Ich **habe** mein Fahrrad **repariert**.
I repaired my bike.

10.24 The perfect: separable verbs (*trennbare Verben*)

Separable verbs have **-ge-** sandwiched in the middle of their past participles. Here are examples for both weak and strong verbs:

aufwachen ⸱⸱⸱⸱⸱⸳ Ich bin um sieben Uhr auf**ge**wacht.
I woke up at 7 o'clock.

ausziehen ⸱⸱⸱⸱⸱⸳ Ich habe meinen Mantel aus**ge**zog**en**.
I took off my coat.

10.25 The perfect: reflexive verbs (*reflexive Verben*)

These all take **haben** in German:

sich **an**ziehen ⸱⸱⸱⸱⸱⸳ Ich **habe mich** schnell **angezogen**.
I got dressed quickly.

10.26   The perfect: irregular verbs (*unregelmäßige Verben*)

These verbs have an irregular past participle. They can be found in the verb list (10.43). These same verbs were also dealt with in 10.16.

bringen   ⋯⋯⋗ Dieter hat uns zum Bahnhof **gebracht**.
Dieter took us to the station.

10.27   The perfect: modal verbs (*Modalverben*)

Modal verbs are not often used in the perfect tense – the simple past is normally used instead – so they will be described here very briefly. Modals are almost always used with another verb. In the perfect, this other verb is the next-to-last word in the clause or sentence. The final word is the modal verb itself – *in the infinitive*. **Haben** (never **sein**) is used.

Ich **habe** dich gestern nicht **besuchen können**.
I couldn't visit you yesterday.

I **habe** nach Berlin **fahren müssen**.
I had to go to Berlin.

When the modal verb is used without another verb, there are special past participles: **gekonnt**, **gemusst**, **gewollt**, **gesollt**, **gedurft** and **gemocht**. These are rare except in the phrase:

Das **habe** ich nicht **gewollt**.
I didn't mean to.

lassen + infinitive (see 10.7c) forms its perfect tense in the same way:

Ich **habe** mir die Haare **schneiden lassen**.
I have had my hair cut.

10.28   The pluperfect tense – *das Plusquamperfekt*

In English, this tense is made up of *had* and a past participle. For example:

I **had** never **seen** that film before.

The pluperfect usually denotes an event further back in the past than other past tenses.

After I **had bought** some bread, I **went** home.

In this example, the pluperfect shows that the buying of the bread took place further back in the past than the going home.

In German, the pluperfect is constructed in a very similar way to the perfect tense. The only difference is that the present tenses of **haben** and **sein** are replaced by their simple past forms (see 10.16). This means that we use **hatte** (or **war** for verbs which take **sein**) *plus* the past participle.

Ich **hatte** den Film noch nie **gesehen**.
I **had** never **seen** that film before.

Ich **war** schon 1982 in Rom **gewesen**.
I **had** already **been** to Rome in 1982.

You will most often need to use the pluperfect in subordinate clauses beginning with **nachdem** (*after*).

> Nachdem **ich** Brot **gekauft hatte**, ging ich nach Hause.
> After **I had bought** some bread, I went home.

> Nachdem **wir** nach New York **geflogen waren**, fuhren wir mit dem Zug nach Washington.
> After **we had flown** to New York, we went by train to Washington.

10.29 Referring to the future

German has a future tense which consists of the present tense of **werden** (see 10.9) *plus* an infinitive (which is sent to the end of the sentence).

> Ich **werde** eines Tages **heiraten**.
> I **shall get married** one day.

However, this future tense is not very often used. Whenever it is already clear that you are talking about the future, you can simply use the present tense:

> Ich fahre jetzt in die Stadt, aber **ich bin** um vier Uhr wieder hier.
> I am going into town now, but **I shall be** back here at four o'clock.

> Morgen **gehen wir** schwimmen.
> Tomorrow **we'll go** swimming.

For more ways of talking about the future, see 12.3.

10.30 The dative used with verbs

German has many verbs and verbal expressions which involve the dative. The main ones are explained below. (For general information on the dative, see 3.5.)

10.30a Verbs with a dative object

With these verbs, the object is in the dative (where you would have expected to find an accusative direct object). Here is a useful list:

antworten + dat.	*to answer someone*
begegnen* + dat.	*to meet by chance*
danken + dat.	*to thank*
erlauben + dat.	*to allow*
folgen* + dat.	*to follow*
gehören + dat.	*to belong*
glauben + dat.	*to believe someone*
helfen + dat.	*to help*
sich nähern + dat.	*to approach*
verbieten + dat.	*to forbid someone to ...*
vergeben + dat.	*to forgive*
verzeihen + dat.	*to pardon, excuse*

*These verbs form the perfect tense with **sein**.

Here are some examples of these in use:

Kannst du **mir** helfen?
Can you help me?

Ich dankte **dem Gepäckträger**.
I thanked the porter.

Der Polizist folgte **dem Dieb**.
The policeman followed the thief.

Peter antwortete **ihr** nicht.
Peter did not answer her.

Wir näherten uns **der Berghütte**.
We approached the mountain hut.

10.30b   *gefallen*

gefallen is often used where we would say *like* in English. However, the German sentence is the opposite way round from the English equivalent.

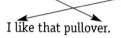

Der Pullover gefällt mir gut.

I like that pullover.

The German sentence says, literally: 'The pullover *appeals to me*'. In German, the *thing* that you like is the *subject* (nominative), and the word (or words) for the person is put in the *dative* case.

Gefällt dir der Rock, Mutti?   Ja, **er gefällt mir** sehr gut.
Do you like that skirt, Mum?   Yes, **I like it** very much.

In this last example, **er** is used for *it*, because we are referring back to **der Rock** (m.). This table shows the various possibilities in singular and plural:

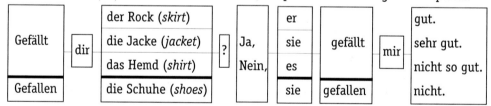

Gefällt	dir	der Rock (*skirt*)	?	Ja,	er	gefällt	mir	gut.
		die Jacke (*jacket*)			sie			sehr gut.
		das Hemd (*shirt*)		Nein,	es			nicht so gut.
Gefallen		die Schuhe (*shoes*)			sie	gefallen		nicht.

A dative noun as well as a pronoun can be used, as in the next example:

Dieses Buch gefällt **meinen Eltern** nicht.
My parents do not like this book.

NOTE that **gefallen** is a strong verb. The simple past is **gefiel** and the perfect is **hat gefallen**.

For more ways of expressing liking in German, see 12.4.

10.30c   *schmecken*

schmecken means *to taste*. It is used for discussing the flavour of food, and it behaves in very much the same way as **gefallen** (see 10.30b above). The food is the subject of the German sentence. The word (or words) for the person who is enjoying (or not enjoying) the food is put in the dative.

Wie **schmeckt dir der Schinken**?
How do you like the ham?
(literally: How does the ham taste to you?)

Er schmeckt mir sehr gut, danke.
It tastes very good (to me).

There need not be a person mentioned:

Dieser Kuchen schmeckt ausgezeichnet.
This cake tastes excellent.

Diese Kartoffeln schmecken furchtbar.
These potatoes taste awful.

When used on its own, **schmecken** implies *to taste **good***.

Hat es geschmeckt?
Did you enjoy it? / Did it taste good?

Das schmeckt!
That tastes good!

10.30d How to talk about how people are

The formula for this is: **es geht** + a person in the dative:

Wie geht's [= geht es] **dir**?
How are you?

Wie geht's **deinem Bruder**?
How's your brother?

Wie geht's **deinen Eltern**?
How are your parents?

Es geht **mir** gut.
I am fine.

Es geht **mir** jetzt besser.
I am better now.

Meiner Oma geht es nicht so gut.
My grandma is not very well.

See also 12.2.

 Do not say or write: ~~Ich bin gut~~, ~~Meine Oma ist besser~~, etc. These are wrong!

10.30e Other health and 'state' expressions with the word (or words) for the person in the dative

This table shows these and the way they work:

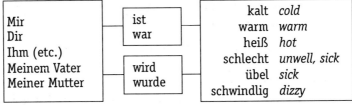

Mir		ist		kalt	*cold*
Dir		war		warm	*warm*
Ihm (etc.)				heiß	*hot*
Meinem Vater		wird		schlecht	*unwell, sick*
Meiner Mutter		wurde		übel	*sick*
				schwindlig	*dizzy*

Mir ist kalt.
I'm cold.

Mir wird kalt.
I'm getting cold.

Ist **dir** warm?
Are you warm?

Ihm war heiß.
He was hot.

Ihr wurde schwindlig.
She became/got dizzy.

Meinem Bruder ist schlecht.
My brother feels funny/sick.

 This is, more or less, a fixed list. These are the only adjectives that function in this way. Do not say or write, for instance, ~~Mir ist krank~~. This is not German!

10.31   Verbs with prepositions

Many verbs, both English and German, have one or more prepositions associated with them. English examples are:

| to wait for | ⟶ | I **waited for** the bus. |
| to think of | ⟶ | I **thought of** you. |

The verb and its preposition form a fixed phrase. German has many of these verbs followed by prepositions. Here is a useful selection:

denken an + acc. *to think of*	⟶	Ich **dachte an dich.** I thought of you.
sich erinnern an + acc. *to remember*	⟶	Ich **erinnere mich an ihn.** I remember him.
fragen nach + dat. *to ask about*	⟶	Ich **fragte nach ihrem Mann.** I asked about her husband.
sich interessieren für + acc. *to be interested in*	⟶	Ich **interessiere mich für Sport.** I'm interested in sport.
schreiben an + acc. *to write to*	⟶	Ich **schrieb an Maria.** I wrote to Maria.
warten auf + acc. *to wait for*	⟶	Ich **wartete auf den Bus.** I waited for the bus.

10.32   Infinitives: with and without *zu*

German clauses and sentences often have an infinitive at (or near) the end. This infinitive may or may not have **zu** before it.

10.32a   Infinitives without *zu*

There is no **zu** when the previous verb is:

* **a modal verb** (see 10.8)

   Ich **will** nach Hause **fahren.**
   I want to go home.

* **werden** (forming the future – see 10.29)

   Ich **werde** nach Hause **fahren.**
   I shall go home.

* **gehen**   *to go and do something*

   Wir **gehen** morgen **einkaufen.**
   We're going shopping tomorrow.

- **sehen/hören** *to see or hear something happen*

  Ich **hörte** ihn ins Haus **kommen**.
  I heard him come into the house.

- **lassen** *to have something done for oneself* (see 10.7c)

  Ich **lasse** mir die Haare **schneiden**.
  I'm having my hair cut.

Infinitives without **zu** are also used in commands and instructions (see 10.10.4).

Remember that in subordinate clauses (9.8), the infinitive is no longer the last word in the clause:

  Ich fahre in die Stadt, weil ich einen neuen Pullover **kaufen muss**.
  I'm going into town because I have to buy a new pullover.

10.32b Infinitives with *zu*

Whenever infinitives are used in situations other than those listed in 10.32a, **zu** is needed directly before the infinitive. There are many verbs and verb phrases which are followed by **zu** and an infinitive. These are just a few examples:

- **versuchen** *to try*

  Ich **versuchte** das Fenster **zu öffnen**.
  I tried to open the window.

- **beschließen** *to decide*

  Ich **habe beschlossen**, Physik **zu studieren**.
  I've decided to study physics.

- **Lust haben** *to feel like*

  Ich **habe keine Lust**, ins Kino **zu gehen**.
  I don't feel like going to the cinema.

- **sich darauf freuen** *to look forward to doing something*

  Ich **freue mich darauf**, dich **zu besuchen**.
  I'm looking forward to visiting you.

When **zu** is used with the infinitive of a separable verb, the **zu** is sandwiched into the middle:

  Ich habe vor, heute Abend fern**zu**sehen.
  I'm intending to watch TV this evening.

Punctuation before zu + infinitive

There is normally a comma before the part of the sentence related to **zu** + infinitive, although this is now officially optional.

  Ich habe beschlossen(,) Physik zu studieren.

One clause at a time

It sounds more natural to complete the verb already begun before starting a **zu** + infinitive clause:

  Es **fing an** zu regnen.
  It started to rain.

  Das Baby **hörte auf** zu weinen.
  The baby stopped crying.

BUT it is not wrong to leave the **an** and **auf** to the end of the sentence.

statt zu + infinitive and *ohne zu* + infinitive

statt zu + infinitive (sometimes **anstatt zu** + infinitive) means *instead of doing something*:

> **Statt zu halten**, fuhr Karsten weiter.
> **Instead of stopping**, Karsten drove on.

ohne zu + infinitive means *without doing something*:

> An der Ampel fuhr er bei Rot durch, **ohne** den Polizisten **zu sehen**.
> At the traffic-lights he went through on red, **without seeing** the policeman.

10.33 *um zu* + infinitive

This is the German way of saying *in order to do something*, as in this table:

Ich bleibe zu Hause, *I'm staying at home*	**um zu** arbeiten	*in order to work*
	um Schach **zu** spielen	*in order to play chess*
	um fern**zu**sehen	*in order to watch TV*
	um einen Brief **zu** schreiben	*in order to write a letter*

NOTE that there is a comma separating the **um zu** clause from the rest of the sentence. In the third example, as always, **zu** is sandwiched into the middle of a separable verb. In the second and fourth examples, notice that there can be a direct object (**Schach** and **einen Brief**) sandwiched between **um** and the **zu** + infinitive.

In English, we often leave out the words *in order* and say simply:

> I'm staying at home to work.

However, when the underlying meaning is *in order to*, you must use **um zu** + infinitive in German.

10.34 The passive – *das Passiv*

Active and passive – what are they?

Most sentences are *active*: a subject 'acts', i.e. does an action. For example:

> A policeman arrested the burglar.

Some sentences, including this one, can also be expressed less directly, in the passive, like this:

> The burglar was arrested by a policeman.

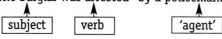

NOTE that the *direct object* of the original active sentence has become the *subject* of the passive sentence:

Active: A policeman arrested **the burglar**.

Passive: **The burglar** was arrested by a policeman.

The subject of the active sentence becomes the 'agent' in a passive sentence. In English, the agent has *by* in front of it: *by a policeman*.

The agent is often simply left out, however:

> The burglar was arrested.

If we translate this example sentence into German, we can see how to construct passive sentences:

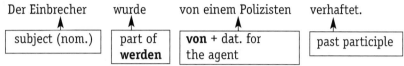

Der Einbrecher   wurde   von einem Polizisten   verhaftet.

| subject (nom.) | part of **werden** | **von** + dat. for the agent | past participle |

This example shows that the passive is formed from these two elements: the relevant tense of **werden** (this is a past tense sentence, so the simple past **wurde** is used) *plus* a past participle (see 10.17) at the end of the clause or sentence.

Here are some examples of the passive with other tenses and verb forms (NOTE the changes in word order):

Present: Diese Kirche **wird** von vielen Touristen **fotografiert**.
           This church **is photographed** by many tourists.

Modal: Dieses Formular **muss** sofort **ausgefüllt werden**.
           This form **must be filled** in immediately.

Perfect: Meine Autoschlüssel **sind gestohlen worden**.
           My car keys **have been stolen**.

The last example is the most complex. It consists of the perfect tense of **werden**, which is shortened from **sind geworden** to **sind worden** in the passive, *plus* the past participle, **gestohlen**.

Finer points of the passive

a   English passive sentences which have no direct German equivalent

Only the *direct object* of an active sentence can become the *subject* of a passive sentence:

> Viele Leute diskutieren **diesen Plan**.
> **Dieser Plan** wird von vielen Leuten diskutiert.

This means that some English sentences – such as the following – have no direct equivalent in German:

> I was given a book.
> He was not believed.

In the first of these, the problem is that *I* was not *given*. In fact, a book was given *to me*. In German this becomes:

> **Mir** wurde ein Buch gegeben.

In the second English sentence, the difficulty lies with the German verb **glauben**. It is one of the verbs which is followed by a dative person (See 10.30a). The translation is:

> Es wurde **ihm** nicht geglaubt
> OR   **Ihm** wurde nicht geglaubt.

In the second version, note that no subject is expressed at all.

b Impersonal passives

Look at these examples:

Es wird gestreikt.	*There's a strike on.*
Heute Abend wird gefeiert.	*There's a celebration tonight.*
Jetzt wird gearbeitet!	*Now it's time for some work.*

These expressions of activity are all based on **es wird**. However, the word **es** is omitted when some other item is placed at the beginning of the sentence.

c *sein* or *werden*?

English-speaking learners usually have to work hard to remember to use **werden** and not **sein** in passive expressions. However, **sein** is sometimes correct. **werden** really means *become* and indicates a process or an activity:

Alle freuten sich, als das Problem **gelöst wurde**.
Everybody was glad when the problem was solved.

This means that everybody was glad *when the solution occurred*. However, the following sentence is also possible:

Alle freuten sich, dass das Problem endlich **gelöst war**.
Everybody was glad that the problem was at last solved.

This means that everybody was glad about the state of affairs *when the solution was already in place*.

10.35 The subjunctive – *der Konjunktiv*

<u>What is the subjunctive?</u>

The subjunctive is a set of verb forms which are needed in certain types of sentence in German. When the subjunctive is used, it lends a touch of uncertainty or wishful thinking to a sentence. However, you do not use the subjunctive whenever you feel like it. It is used in certain situations only, and these are explained in later sections (10.38 Reported speech, 10.39 Conditional sentences, 10.40 Other uses of the subjunctive).

The subjunctive has two main 'tenses'. (I put the word in inverted commas because, unlike ordinary tense, the 'tenses' of the subjunctive are not connected with different times.) These two tenses are *subjunctive I* and *subjunctive II*. These are sometimes known, rather confusingly, as the present and past subjunctive.

10.36 Subjunctive I

To make subjunctive I, take the stem of the verb and add the subjunctive endings. As an example, here is the verb **fahren** (*to go*):

ich	fahr**e**		wir	fahr**en**
du	fahr**est**		ihr	fahr**et**
er/sie/es	fahr**e** [no **t** ending]		Sie/sie	fahr**en**

NOTE that all the subjunctive endings contain **e**. The **ich** and **er/sie/es** parts are always identical in the subjunctive.

fahren is a strong verb which modifies its stem in the ordinary present tense (see 10.5). There is *no* stem modification in the subjunctive.

Only one verb has an irregular subjunctive I. This verb is **sein** (*to be*):

ich	**sei**	wir	**seien**
du	**seist/seiest**	ihr	**seiet**
er/sie/es	**sei**	Sie/sie	**seien**

10.37 Subjunctive II

For weak verbs (see 10.13), subjunctive II is identical to the ordinary simple past **ich spielte**, **ich wohnte**, **ich arbeitete**.

For strong verbs, take the ordinary simple past form, add the subjunctive endings (the same ones as for subjunctive I), as in the example of **gehen** (*to go*):

ich	ging**e**	wir	ging**en**
du	ging**est**	ihr	ging**et**
er/sie/es	ging**e**	Sie/sie	ging**en**

This is formed from the simple past of **gehen**, which is **ging**.

If possible – i.e. if the vowel in the simple past stem is **a**, **o** or **u** – add Umlaut. This happens, for example, with **wäre** (from **war**), **führe** (from **fuhr**) and **käme** (from **kam**).

Here are the subjunctive II forms of modal verbs:

können	····⟩	ich **könnte**
müssen	····⟩	ich **müsste**
wollen	····⟩	ich **wollte**
sollen	····⟩	ich **sollte**
dürfen	····⟩	ich **dürfte**
mögen	····⟩	ich **möchte**

Compare these with their ordinary simple past forms in 10.15.

 NOTE that **wollte** and **sollte** never have Umlaut.

Common irregular verbs:

haben	····⟩	ich **hätte**
wissen	····⟩	ich **wüsste**
werden	····⟩	ich **würde**
bringen	····⟩	ich **brächte**

Compare these with their ordinary simple past forms in 10.16.

10.38 Reported speech (*indirekte Rede*)

<u>What is reported speech?</u>

Reported speech, as the name suggests, is the reporting of someone's words:

> He said that he had no money.
> She said her father was ill.
> He asked whether we could help him.

The above are reported versions of these original words:

'I have no money.'
'My father is ill.'
'Can you help me?'

In German, the subjunctive is the most common way of showing that someone's words are being reported. If we translate the first English example above into German, we get:

Er sagte, dass er kein Geld habe.

habe is a subjunctive I form. Do *not* use the simple past (**hatte**) here.

10.38a Subjunctive I or subjunctive II in reported speech?

You can use either! The important thing is to use a *distinctively subjunctive* form – i.e. *not* one which is identical with either the ordinary present or simple past tenses. These examples will make the point clear:

Peter sagte, dass er krank **sei/wäre**. Peter said that he **was** ill.	both verb forms are distinctively subjunctive, so both are possible
Peter sagte, dass er in London **wohne**. Peter said that he **lived** in London.	**wohnte** would be identical with the simple past, so it cannot be used

In written German, there is a preference for subjunctive I in reported speech, when this provides a distinctive form.

Study these further examples to see how to construct various types of reported speech:

Petra sagte, dass sie nicht **mitkommen könne/könnte**.
Petra said that she **could** not **come with us**.

Peter sagte, dass er den Film nicht **gesehen habe/hätte**.
Peter said that **he had** not **seen** the film.

Petra sagte, dass sie mit dem Taxi **gefahren sei/wäre**.
Petra said that she **had gone** by taxi.

Peter sagte, dass er ein Auto **kaufen werde/würde**.
Peter said that he **was going to buy** a car.

The last of the above examples shows what to do when the original words referred to the future. (Here they must have been: *'I am going to buy a car'*.) In German, **werde** or **würde** (*would*) is used with an infinitive.

Leaving out *dass*

In all of the above examples, **dass** could have been left out. When this happens, there is still a comma, but the verb is not sent to the end:

Peter sagte, er **sei/wäre** krank.
Peter said he **was** ill.

10.38b   Reported questions

In reported questions, **ob** is used for *whether* or *if* (*not* **wenn**!), but the ordinary question words are often needed instead (see Chapter 5):

Petra fragte, **ob** ich Geschwister **hätte**. [not **habe**, which is not distinctive]
Petra asked **whether/if** I **had** any brothers or sisters.

Peter fragte mich, **ob** ich zur Party **gehen möchte**. [**möchte** = would like to]
Peter asked me **whether** I **would like to go** to the party.

Petra fragte, **ob** wir ihr **helfen könnten**. [**können** would not be distinctive]
Petra asked **whether** we **could help** her.

Peter fragte, **wann** der Zug **ankommen würde**.
Peter asked **when** the train **would / was going to arrive**.

Petra fragte, **wo** die Polizeiwache **sei/wäre**.
Petra asked **where** the police station **was**.

10.38c   Reported commands

She asked me to open the door, etc.

When the verb is *ask*, German uses the verb **bitten** with a similar sentence construction to the English one:

Sie **bat** mich, die **Tür aufzumachen**.
She **asked** me **to open** the door.

She told me to open the door, etc.

With other verbs (such as *tell*), a different construction is needed in German:

Sie **sagte mir**, ich **sollte** [OR: **müsste**] die Tür **aufmachen**.
She told me to open the door.

Leaving out *dass*

Sie sagte mir, ich sollte/müsste die Tür aufmachen.

The German sentence literally says: *She said to me that I should* [OR: *had to*] *open the door.*

10.38d   Reported speech without the subjunctive

When the verb of saying (e.g. **sagen**, **fragen**) is in a tense other than the past, ordinary tenses are often used instead of the subjunctive. In spoken German, the subjunctive is often avoided even after **sagte** and **fragte**. However, the tenses used are not the past tenses that we use in English:

Peter hat mir gesagt, dass er krank **ist**.
Peter told me that he **was** ill.

German uses the same tense as the original words (e.g. *'I am ill'* – present tense).

10.39   Conditional sentences

What are conditional sentences?

These are sentences which involve *if* in English. There are two types: 'real' conditional sentences and 'unreal' conditional sentences.

So-called 'real' conditional sentences are about things which are perfectly likely to happen:

If I **have** enough money, I'**ll buy** a house.

This is straightforward in German:

Wenn ich genug Geld **habe**, **kaufe** ich ein Haus.

The verbs are in the ordinary present tense.

'Unreal' conditional sentences are about things which are very unlikely to happen. Often, they describe wishful thinking:

If I **had** enough money, I **would buy** a house.

The point here is that the speaker has *not* got enough money and in fact can*not* buy a house. He or she is just imagining what *might be*.

In German, unreal conditional sentences require *subjunctive II in both clauses*. Subjunctive I *cannot* be used! In theory, any subjunctive II forms can be used, but in practice only the most frequently used verbs are normally put into subjunctive II. These verbs are **sein** (*to be*), **haben** (*to have*) and the modal verbs (see 10.37 for their subjunctive II forms). For other verbs, the subjunctive II form is replaced by **würde** + infinitive. Study these examples:

Wenn ich reich **wäre**, **würde ich** einen Porsche kaufen.
If I **were** rich I **would buy** a Porsche.

Wenn ich eine Million Mark **gewinnen würde**, **wäre** ich sehr glücklich.
If I **won** a million Marks, I **would be** very happy.

Wenn ich viel Geld **hätte**, **könnte** ich eine Weltreise **machen**.
If I had a lot of money I **could** [OR: **would be able to**] **go** on a world tour.

Ich **wäre** sehr dankbar, wenn Sie mir **helfen könnten**.
I **would be** very grateful if you **could help** me.

REMEMBER: verb forms based on subjunctive II are used in *both* clauses.

Omission of *wenn*

In English we sometimes omit the word *if*, and instead 'invert' the verb and the subject at the beginning of the sentence:

Had I the time [= If I had the time], I would take up painting.

This possibility exists in German too and is used much more widely than in English:

Arbeitet man nicht [= Wenn man nicht arbeitet], bleibt man sitzen.
If you don't work, you have to repeat the year.

konnte or *könnte*?

Both of these mean *could*, but they are not the same!

konnte is the simple past tense and means *was able to*:

Gestern **konnte** ich **nicht** schwimmen gehen.
Yesterday I **couldn't** [= **was not able to**] go swimming.

könnte is subjunctive II and means *would be able to* or *might be able to*:

Wenn das Wetter schön **wäre**, **könnte** ich schwimmen gehen.
If the weather were nice, I **could** [= **would be able to**] go swimming.

Könnten Sie mir bitte helfen?
Could you [= **Might you be able to**] help me?

10.40 Other uses of the subjunctive

Here are some other uses of the subjunctive that you are likely to meet.

10.40a Subjunctive II as a polite form

hätte, **wäre** and **könnte** are often used as polite forms. They seem less abrupt than the ordinary present tenses of **haben**, **sein** or **können** in examples such as these:

> Das **wäre** alles. [= Das **ist** alles.]
> That's all.

> **Hättest** [= **Hast**] du Lust mitzukommen?
> Do you feel like coming with us?

> **Könntest** [= **Kannst**] du mir helfen?
> Could/Can you help me?

10.40b *als ob* (*as if*)

als ob does not always require the subjunctive, but it is normal in past tense sentences:

> Er sah aus, **als ob** er krank **sei/wäre**.
> He looked **as if** he **was/were** ill.

10.40c How to express *could have* and *should have*

These two examples show how to do this using **hätte** + infinitive + **können/sollen**:

> Du **hättest** gestern **mitkommen können**.
> You **could have come with** us yesterday.

> Du **hättest** gestern **mitkommen sollen**.
> You **should have come with** us yesterday.

10.41 Other points about verbs

10.41a How to express *there is* and *there are*

For *there is* and *there are*, German usually uses **es gibt** + accusative:

> **Es gibt** viel Verkehr heute.
> **There's** a lot of traffic today.

> **Es gibt** Fisch zum Abendessen.
> **There's** fish for supper.

> Was **gibt es** heute im Fernsehen?
> What **is there** on TV today?

To indicate that something is in a specific place, **es ist/sind** + nominative is used:

Es ist ein Mann an der Tür.
There's a man at the door.

Es sind zwei Hefte auf dem Tisch.
There are two exercise books on the table.

10.41b   To want somebody to do something

wollen (see 10.8) is used when the subject of the sentence wants to do something:

> **Ich will** das Mittagessen **kochen.**
> **I want to cook** the lunch.

When *someone wants somebody else to do something*, it is expressed like this:

> **Ich will, dass** Martin das Mittagessen **kocht.**
> **I want Martin to cook** the lunch.
> (literally: I want that Martin cooks the lunch.)

10.42   English verbs with more than one German equivalent

Here, in alphabetical order, are some of the common English verbs that cause problems for learners of German because they have more than one German equivalent. (Verbs marked * take **sein** in the perfect tense – see 10.22. Separable prefixes are shown in **bold italic** type in this section.)

agree

to share someone's opinion, to agree with someone	*überein*stimmen **mit** + dat.	Ich **stimme mit dir überein.** I agree with you.
	OR: **Recht geben** + dat.	Ich **gebe dir Recht.** I agree with you.
	OR: **finden/meinen** + **auch**	Das **finde/meine** ich **auch.** I agree.
to agree to something	*zu*stimmen + dat.	Ich **stimmte seinem Plan zu.** I agreed to his plan.
to have no objection, to consent (to something)	**einverstanden sein** (**mit** + dat.)	Alle **waren mit seinem Plan einverstanden.** Everybody agreed with his plan.
to be of one mind	**sich** (dat.) **einig sein**	Alle **waren sich einig**, dass der Plan gut war. Everybody agreed that the plan was good.
to agree on something (fairly easily)	**sich einigen auf** + acc.	Wir **einigten uns auf eine Party** am 6. August. We agreed on a party on 6 August.
to agree on something (with effort)	**vereinbaren** + acc.	Sie **vereinbarten einen Friedensplan.** They agreed on a peace plan.

answer

to answer a person	**antworten** + dat.	Er **antwortete ihr** nicht. He did not answer her.
to answer a thing	**antworten auf** + acc.	Er **antwortete auf meinen Brief.**
	OR: **beantworten** + acc.	Er **beantwortete meinen Brief.** He answered my letter.

ask

to ask a question	**fragen** + acc.	Ich **fragte ihn**, wo er wohnte. I asked him where he lived.
to ask after/about	**fragen nach** + dat.	Ich **fragte nach ihrer Mutter**. I asked about her mother.
to ask for something	**bitten** + acc. **um** + acc.	Ich **bat ihn um eine Briefmarke**. I asked him for a stamp.
to ask someone to do something	**bitten** + acc. **zu** + inf.	Ich **bat sie mich zu besuchen**. I asked her to visit me.

go

to go on foot	**gehen***	Wir **gingen** durch den Wald. We went through the forest.
to go in a vehicle	**fahren***	Wir **fuhren** nach Frankreich. We went to France.

BUT **gehen** is used in the special meaning *to go and live somewhere,* as in:

Mein Bruder **ist** nach Frankreich **gegangen**.
My brother has gone to (live in) France.

know

to know information	**wissen**	Die Antwort **weiß** ich nicht. I don't know the answer.
to be acquainted with	**kennen**	Ich **kenne** ihn nicht. I don't know him.

leave

to leave something somewhere	**lassen**/*zurück***lassen**	Ich **ließ** mein Buch zu Hause (**zurück**). I left my book (behind) at home.
to leave someone *or* somewhere	**verlassen** + acc. (*must* have a direct object)	Ich **verließ das Haus** um acht. I left the house at eight.
to depart, to set off	*ab***fahren***/ *los***fahren***	Der Zug **fuhr** um acht Uhr **ab**. The train left at eight o'clock. Wir **fuhren** gleich **los**. We set off straight away·

like

See 12.4g, and for **gefallen** see also 10.30b.

live

to live one's life	**leben**	Bismarck **lebte** im 19. Jahrhundert. Bismarck lived in the 19th century.
to reside somewhere	**wohnen**	Wir **wohnen** in einem Dorf. We live in a village.

look

to have an appearance	*aussehen*	Du **siehst** schick **aus**. You look smart.
to look with one's eyes	**sehen/schauen** (also, in con- versation: **gucken**)	**Sieh/Schau** mal! **Guck** mal! Just look!
to look at	*ansehen*	Der Polizist **sah** mich **an**. The policeman looked at me.
to look at something	**sehen auf** + acc.	Er **sah auf seine Uhr**. He looked at his watch.

mean

to try to say, to give/ hold an opinion	**meinen** (the subject must be a person)	Was **meinst** du? What do you mean?
to be the definition of	**heißen**	Was **heißt** „Tisch" auf Englisch? What does 'Tisch' mean in English?
to be the significance of	**bedeuten**	Was **bedeutet** diese Entscheidung? What does this decision mean?

meet

most meanings of *meet*	**treffen** + acc. (*must* have a direct object)	Jan **traf Ute** vor dem Kino. Jan met Ute outside the cinema.
to meet one another	**sich treffen**	Wo **treffen** wir **uns**? Where shall we meet (one another)?
to meet by chance	**begegnen*** + dat.	Udo **ist mir** heute **begegnet**. Udo met me (by chance) today.
to collect / call for someone	*abholen*	Jutta **holte** mich am Bahnhof **ab**. Jutta met me at the station.
to make someone's acquaintance	**kennen lernen**	Ich freue mich darauf, deine Eltern **kennen zu lernen**. I'm looking forward to meeting your parents.

prefer
See 12.4.

put

to lay something down	**legen** (regular!)	Ich **legte** das Buch auf den Tisch. I put the book on the table.
to stand something up	**stellen**	Ich **stellte** das Glas auf den Tisch. I put the glass on the table.
to insert	**stecken**	Ich **steckte** den Brief in den Umschlag. I put the letter in the envelope.
general meanings of *put*	**tun**	Ich **tat** Fett in die Pfanne. I put some fat in the frying-pan.

Do not confuse **legen** and **liegen**.
Legen means *put* as shown above.
Liegen means *lie* and shows a position.

Das Buch **liegt** auf dem Tisch.
The book is (lying) on the table.

say

to utter words	**sagen**	Er **sagte**: „Hallo!" He said, 'Hello.'
to be written	**heißen**	In der Zeitung **heißt** es, dass es einen Unfall gegeben hat. It says in the paper that there has been an accident.
	OR: **stehen**	In der Zeitung **steht**, dass es einen Unfall gegeben hat. It says in the paper that there has been an accident.

sit

to sit down (motion)	sich *hin*setzen / **sich setzen** (regular)	Ich **setzte mich** auf das Sofa (**hin**). I sat down on the sofa.
to sit (position)	**sitzen** (strong)	Ich **saß** immer in der Ecke. I always sat in the corner.

spend

to spend money	*aus*geben	Gestern **gab** ich hundert Mark **aus**. Yesterday I spent a hundred Marks.
to spend time	**verbringen**	Ich **verbrachte** die Ferien in Rom. I spent the holidays in Rome.

stay

to remain	**bleiben***	Ich **blieb** zwei Tage in Berlin. I stayed in Berlin for two days.
to live somewhere for a while	**wohnen**	Ich **wohnte** in einem Hotel. I stayed in a hotel.
to stay overnight	**übernachten**	Ich **übernachtete** in einem Hotel. I stayed overnight in a hotel.

stop

to stop travelling	**halten/anhalten**	Warum **hat** der Zug hier **gehalten**? Why has the train stopped here?
to stop walking	*stehen*bleiben*	Er **blieb** vor unserem Haus **stehen**. He stopped outside our house.
to make someone else stop	*an*halten	Ein Polizist **hielt** uns **an**. A policeman stopped us.
to cease an activity	*auf*hören **zu** + inf.	Wir **hörten auf** zu arbeiten. We stopped working.
to prevent someone from doing something	*ab*halten + acc. **davon, zu** + inf.	Er **hielt** mich **davon ab**, ins Kino **zu gehen**. He stopped me from going to the cinema.
to come to an end	*auf*hören	Der Regen **hat aufgehört**. The rain has stopped.

take

basic meanings of *take*	**nehmen**	Ich **nahm** das Buch von dem Tisch. I took the book from the table.
		Ich **nahm** den Bus. I took the bus.
to transport, to accompany	**bringen**	Er **brachte** mich nach Hause. He took me home.
to take time	**brauchen**	Ich **brauche** zwei Stunden, um meine Hausaufgaben zu machen. It takes me two hours to do my homework. (literally: 'I need ...')

think

to use one's brain	**denken**	Sie **denkt** viel. She thinks a lot.
to have thoughts about something/someone	**denken an** + acc.	Ich habe gestern **an dich gedacht**. I thought of you yesterday.
to consider something, to weigh something up.	**sich** (dat.) **überlegen** + acc.	Ich habe **mir deinen Plan überlegt**. I have thought about your plan.
to ponder something, to mull something over	*nach*denken **über** + acc.	Ich habe **über deinen Plan nachgedacht**. I have thought (carefully) about your plan.
to believe	**glauben**	Ich **glaube**, dass er recht hat. I think he's right.
to hold an opinion (about something)	**meinen**	Was **meinst** du? What do you think?
to hold an opinion about something	**meinen zu** + dat. / **halten von** + dat. / **denken über** + acc./ **finden** + acc.	Was **meinst** du **zu meiner Idee**? Was **hältst** du **von meiner Idee**? Was **denkst** du **über meine Idee**? Wie **findest** du **meine Idee**? What do you think of my idea?

wake up

| to stop sleeping | *auf*wachen* /
wach werden* | Ich **bin** um acht Uhr **aufgewacht** / **wach geworden**.
I woke up at eight o'clock. |
| to wake someone else up | **wecken** | Ich **weckte** meinen Bruder um neun.
I woke my brother up at nine. |

10.43 Verb list

This is a list of all the strong and irregular verbs you are likely to meet.

The most essential verbs for speaking and writing your own German are marked with a bullet (•). Many of the most common separable and inseparable verbs have been included on the list, but there was not room for them all. For those which are not listed, look up the basic verb. For example, to find out how *auf*schlagen works, look up schlagen. (Separable prefixes – see 10.6 – are shown in **bold** type in this section.)

From the four forms given here, all the other verb forms can be worked out.

	Infinitive	Present tense (er/sie/es form)	Simple past tense (er/sie/es form)	Perfect tense (er/sie/es form)	English meaning
A	**ab**biegen	biegt...ab	bog...ab	ist abgebogen	*to turn off (a road)*
•	**ab**fahren	fährt...ab	fuhr...ab	ist abgefahren	*to depart*
•	**ab**waschen	wäscht...ab	wusch...ab	hat abgewaschen	*to wash up*
	anbieten	bietet...an	bot...an	hat angeboten	*to offer*
•	**an**fangen	fängt...an	fing...an	hat angefangen	*to start*
•	**an**kommen	kommt...an	kam...an	ist angekommen	*to arrive*
•	**an**rufen	ruft...an	rief...an	hat angerufen	*to ring someone up*
•	**an**ziehen	zieht...an	zog...an	hat angezogen	*to put on (clothes)*
	aufheben	hebt...auf	hob...auf	hat aufgehoben	*to pick something up; to keep*
•	**auf**stehen	steht...auf	stand...auf	ist aufgestanden	*to get up*
•	**aus**geben	gibt...aus	gab...aus	hat ausgegeben	*to spend (money)*
•	**aus**sehen	sieht...aus	sah...aus	hat ausgesehen	*to look, to appear*
•	**aus**steigen	steigt...aus	stieg...aus	ist ausgestiegen	*to get off/out*
•	**aus**ziehen	zieht...aus	zog...aus	hat ausgezogen	*to take off (clothes)*
B	backen	bäckt/backt	backte	hat gebacken	*to bake*
	befehlen	befiehlt	befahl	hat befohlen	*to order (someone to do something)*
•	beginnen	beginnt	begann	hat begonnen	*to begin*
	behalten	behält	behielt	hat behalten	*to keep*
	beißen	beißt	biss	hat gebissen	*to bite*
•	bekommen	bekommt	bekam	hat bekommen	*to get, to receive*
•	beschließen	beschließt	beschloss	hat beschlossen	*to decide*
•	beschreiben	beschreibt	beschrieb	hat beschrieben	*to describe*
	besitzen	besitzt	besaß	hat besessen	*to own*
	biegen	biegt	bog	hat gebogen	*to bend*
	bieten	bietet	bot	hat geboten	*to offer*
	binden	bindet	band	hat gebunden	*to tie*
•	bitten	bittet	bat	hat gebeten	*to ask*
	blasen	bläst	blies	hat geblasen	*to blow*
•	bleiben	bleibt	blieb	ist geblieben	*to stay, to remain*
	braten	brät	briet	hat gebraten	*to fry, to roast*
•	brechen	bricht	brach	hat gebrochen	*to break, to vomit*
	brennen	brennt	brannte	hat gebrannt	*to burn, be on fire*
•	bringen	bringt	brachte	hat gebracht	*to bring, take*
D	denken	denkt	dachte	hat gedacht	*to think*
•	dürfen	darf	durfte	hat (inf.) dürfen	*to be allowed to* (see 10.8)
E	• **ein**laden	lädt...ein	lud...ein	hat eingeladen	*to invite*
	• **ein**schlafen	schläft...ein	schlief...ein	ist eingeschlafen	*to go to sleep*

Infinitive	Present tense (er/sie/es form)	Simple past tense (er/sie/es form)	Perfect tense (er/sie/es form)	English meaning
• **ein**steigen	steigt...ein	stieg...ein	ist eingestiegen	*to get in/on*
empfangen	empfängt	empfing	hat empfangen	*to receive*
empfehlen	empfiehlt	empfahl	hat empfohlen	*to recommend*
sich entscheiden	sich entscheidet	entschied sich	hat sich entschieden	*to decide*
sich entschließen	entschließt sich	entschloss sich	hat sich entschlossen	*to make up one's mind*
erhalten	erhält	erhielt	hat erhalten	*to receive*
erkennen	erkennt	erkannte	hat erkannt	*to recognise*
erscheinen	erscheint	erschien	ist erschienen	*to appear*
erschrecken	erschrickt	erschrak	ist erschrocken	*to get a fright*
• essen	isst	aß	hat gegessen	*to eat*
F • fahren	fährt	fuhr	ist gefahren	*to go, to drive* (see 10.22)
• fallen	fällt	fiel	ist gefallen	*to fall*
fangen	fängt	fing	hat gefangen	*to catch*
• **fern**sehen	sieht...fern	sah...fern	hat ferngesehen	*to watch TV*
• finden	findet	fand	hat gefunden	*to find*
• fliegen	fliegt	flog	ist geflogen	*to fly*
fliehen	flieht	floh	ist geflohen	*to flee, to escape*
fließen	fließt	floss	ist geflossen	*to flow*
fressen	frisst	fraß	hat gefressen	*to eat (used when animals eat)*
frieren	friert	fror	hat gefroren	*to freeze, be cold*
G • geben	gibt	gab	hat gegeben	*to give*
• gefallen	gefällt	gefiel	hat gefallen	*to appeal to*
• gehen	geht	ging	ist gegangen	*to go, to walk*
gelingen	gelingt	gelang	ist gelungen	*to succeed*
genießen	genießt	genoss	hat genossen	*to enjoy*
• geschehen	geschieht	geschah	ist geschehen	*to happen*
• gewinnen	gewinnt	gewann	hat gewonnen	*to win*
gießen	gießt	goss	hat gegossen	*to pour, to water, to pour down*
gleiten	gleitet	glitt	ist geglitten	*to slide, to glide*
graben	gräbt	grub	hat gegraben	*to dig*
greifen	greift	griff	hat gegriffen	*to grab, to seize*
H • haben	hat	hatte	hat gehabt	*to have* (see 10.9)
• halten	hält	hielt	hat gehalten	*to hold, to stop*
hängen	hängt	hing	hat gehangen	*to hang*
heben	hebt	hob	hat gehoben	*to raise, to lift*
• heißen	heißt	hieß	hat geheißen	*to mean, to be called*
• helfen	hilft	half	hat geholfen	*to help*
K • kennen	kennt	kannte	hat gekannt	*to know*
klingen	klingt	klang	hat geklungen	*to sound (odd, etc.)*
• kommen	kommt	kam	ist gekommen	*to come*
• können	kann	konnte	hat (inf.) können	*to be able to, can* (see 10.8)
kriechen	kriecht	kroch	ist gekrochen	*to crawl, to creep*
L • lassen	lässt	ließ	hat gelassen	*to leave something somewhere*
• laufen	läuft	lief	ist gelaufen	*to run, to walk*
leiden	leidet	litt	hat gelitten	*to suffer*
leihen	leiht	lieh	hat geliehen	*to lend, to borrow*

Infinitive	Present tense (er/sie/es form)	Simple past tense (er/sie/es form)	Perfect tense (er/sie/es form)	English meaning
• lesen	liest	las	hat gelesen	to read
• liegen	liegt	lag	hat gelegen	to lie (position)
lügen	lügt	log	hat gelogen	to lie (tell lies)
M messen	misst	maß	hat gemessen	to measure
• mögen	mag	mochte	hat gemocht	to like (see 10.8)
• müssen	muss	musste	hat (inf.) müssen	to have to, must (see 10.8)
N • nehmen	nimmt	nahm	hat genommen	to take
nennen	nennt	nannte	hat genannt	to name, to call
P pfeifen	pfeift	pfiff	hat gepfiffen	to whistle
R raten	rät	riet	hat geraten	to advise, to guess
reißen	reißt	riss	hat gerissen	to tear, to rip
reiten	reitet	ritt	hat geritten	to ride (horses)
• rennen	rennt	rannte	ist gerannt	to run
riechen	riecht	roch	hat gerochen	to smell
• rufen	ruft	rief	hat gerufen	to shout, to call
S • scheinen	scheint	schien	hat geschienen	to shine, to seem
schieben	schiebt	schob	hat geschoben	to push
schießen	schießt	schoss	hat geschossen	to shoot
• schlafen	schläft	schlief	hat geschlafen	to sleep
schlagen	schlägt	schlug	hat geschlagen	to hit, to beat, to strike
• schließen	schließt	schloss	hat geschlossen	to close
schmeißen	schmeißt	schmiss	hat geschmissen	to chuck, to throw (informal)
schneiden	schneidet	schnitt	hat geschnitten	to cut
• schreiben	schreibt	schrieb	hat geschrieben	to write
schreien	schreit	schrie	hat geschrien	to scream, to shout
schweigen	schweigt	schwieg	hat geschwiegen	to be silent
• schwimmen	schwimmt	schwamm	ist geschwommen	to swim
• sehen	sieht	sah	hat gesehen	to see
• sein	ist	war	ist gewesen	to be (see 10.9)
• singen	singt	sang	hat gesungen	to sing
sinken	sinkt	sank	ist gesunken	to sink
• sitzen	sitzt	saß	hat gesessen	to sit
• sollen	soll	sollte	hat (inf.) sollen	to be supposed to (see 10.8)
• sprechen	spricht	sprach	hat gesprochen	to speak
springen	springt	sprang	ist gesprungen	to jump
• stehen	steht	stand	hat gestanden	to stand
• stehlen	stiehlt	stahl	hat gestohlen	to steal
steigen	steigt	stieg	ist gestiegen	to climb, to go up
• sterben	stirbt	starb	ist gestorben	to die
stinken	stinkt	stank	hat gestunken	to stink
stoßen	stößt	stieß	hat gestoßen	to push, to shove, to poke
streichen	streicht	strich	hat gestrichen	to stroke, to paint, to cross out
sich streiten	streitet sich	stritt sich	hat sich gestritten	to quarrel
T • tragen	trägt	trug	hat getragen	to carry, to wear
• treffen	trifft	traf	hat getroffen	to meet someone
treiben	treibt	trieb	hat getrieben	to drive, to do (an activity)
treten	tritt	trat	ist getreten	to step
treten	tritt	trat	hat getreten	to kick

Infinitive	Present tense (er/sie/es form)	Simple past tense (er/sie/es form)	Perfect tense (er/sie/es form)	English meaning
• trinken	trinkt	trank	hat getrunken	*to drink*
• tun	tut	tat	hat getan	*to do, to put*

U

überfahren	überfährt	überfuhr	hat überfahren	*to run over someone/something*
übertreiben	übertreibt	übertrieb	hat übertrieben	*to exaggerate*
umziehen	zieht...um	zog...um	ist umgezogen	*to move house*
• sich **um**ziehen	zieht sich...um	zog sich...um	hat sich umgezogen	*to get changed*
unterbrechen	unterbricht	unterbrach	hat unterbrochen	*to interrupt*
unterhalten	unterhält	unterhielt	hat unterhalten	*to entertain*
unterschreiben	unterschreibt	unterschrieb	hat unterschrieben	*to sign*

V̊

verbergen	verbirgt	verbarg	hat verborgen	*to hide something*
verbieten	verbietet	verbot	hat verboten	*to forbid*
• verbringen	verbringt	verbrachte	hat verbracht	*to spend (time)*
• vergessen	vergisst	vergaß	hat vergessen	*to forget*
vergleichen	vergleicht	verglich	hat verglichen	*to compare*
• verlassen	verlässt	verließ	hat verlassen	*to leave someone/somewhere*
• verlieren	verliert	verlor	hat verloren	*to lose*
vermeiden	vermeidet	vermied	hat vermieden	*to avoid*
verschlafen	verschläft	verschlief	hat verschlafen	*to oversleep*
verschreiben	verschreibt	verschrieb	hat verschrieben	*to prescribe*
verschwinden	verschwindet	verschwand	ist verschwunden	*to disappear*
versprechen	verspricht	versprach	hat versprochen	*to promise*
• verstehen	versteht	verstand	hat verstanden	*to understand*
verzeihen	verzeiht	verzieh	hat verziehen	*to pardon, to excuse*
vorschlagen	schlägt...vor	schlug...vor	hat vorgeschlagen	*to suggest*

W

wachsen	wächst	wuchs	ist gewachsen	*to grow*
• waschen	wäscht	wusch	hat gewaschen	*to wash*
• werden	wird	wurde	ist geworden	*to become* (see 10.9)
werfen	wirft	warf	hat geworfen	*to throw*
• wiegen	wiegt	wog	hat gewogen	*to weigh*
• wissen	weiß	wusste	hat gewusst	*to know* (see 10.9)
• wollen	will	wollte	hat (inf.) wollen	*to want to* (see 10.8)

Z

zerbrechen	zerbricht	zerbrach	hat zerbrochen	*to break, to smash*
ziehen	zieht	zog	hat gezogen	*to pull*
zugreifen	greift...zu	griff...zu	hat zugegriffen	*to help oneself*
zusammenstoßen	stößt...zusammen	stieß...zusammen	ist zusammengestoßen	*to collide, to crash*
zwingen	zwingt	zwang	hat gezwungen	*to force, to compel*

11 Alphabet, spelling and punctuation

11.1 The alphabet

The German alphabet is the same as the English one. Here are the names of the letters to use when spelling aloud. There is no official spelling for the names of the letters, but those given here will give the correct names if they are pronounced like German words.

A	Ah	G	Geh	M	Emm	S	Ess	Y	Ypsilon
B	Beh	H	Hah	N	Enn	T	Teh	Z	Tzett
C	Zeh	I	Ih	O	Oh	U	Uh		
D	Deh	J	Jot	P	Peh	V	Fau		
E	Eh	K	Kah	Q	Kuh	W	Weh		
F	Eff	L	Ell	R	Err	X	Icks		

The double **s** symbol (**ß**) is called **Eszett**, and vowels with Umlaut are called:

Ä	Äh	Ö	Öh	Ü	Üh

To say, for example, *double P* in German, say **zwei P** or **Doppel-P**.

11.2 Capital letters

Do not forget that all German nouns must be given a capital letter. However, adjectives do not have capitals:

Wir haben einen **d**eutschen **W**agen.
We have a **G**erman **c**ar.

11.3 *ß (Eszett)*

These are the rules for when to write **ß** and when to write **ss**:

Rule 1: Always write **ss**, *except after long vowels, where ß is used instead*:

Flu**ss** (*river*) has a short U.
Fu**ß** (*foot*) has a long U.

Rule 2: In capital letters, **ß** is not normally used, so we write **SS**:

FLU**SS**, FU**SS**.

NOTE that some strong and irregular verbs have **ß** in some parts and **ss** in others. For example:

verge**ss**en, vergi**ss**t (short vowels)
verga**ß** (long A)

11.4 German punctuation

. Punkt

, Komma

: Doppelpunkt

; Strichpunkt/Semikolon

! Ausrufezeichen/Ausrufungszeichen

? Fragezeichen

– Gedankenstrich

„" Anführungszeichen/Anführungsstriche/
Gänsefüßchen

NOTE how direct speech is punctuated:

Hans fragte: „Wie heißt du? "
„Wie heißt du? ", fragte Hans.
Petra sagte: „Ich komme aus Berlin."
„Ich komme aus Berlin", sagte Petra.
„Ich komme", sagte Petra, „aus Berlin."

11.5 When to use commas

Commas are required between main and subordinate clauses. The rules can be found in sections 9.7b, 9.8, 9.9, 10.32b and 10.33.

11.6 Abbreviations

There are hundreds of abbreviations used in German, as there are in English, but here are just a few that you will frequently come across.

bzw.	=	beziehungsweise	*or as the case may be*
d.h.	=	das heißt	*that is / i.e.*
usw.	=	und so weiter	*and so on / etc.*
z.B.	=	zum Beispiel	*for example / e.g.*

12 How to say it

Notes

1 For *you*, **du** is mostly used here. Often, of course, you will need to use the **Sie** form. (See 4.3.)

2 Words in brackets ( ) are optional – they may be put in or left out.

3 Words divided by a stroke (/) show possible variations.

4 Words *in italics* in this section are there purely as an example, to show how a phrase or structure is used in sentences.

12.1 Language problems

12.1a How to show you don't understand

Bitte?	Pardon?
Ich verstehe nicht.	I don't understand.
Ich habe das/dich nicht verstanden.	I didn't understand that/you.
Ich verstehe nicht, was du meinst.	I don't understand what you mean.

12.1b How to ask for things to be repeated

Bitte? / Wie bitte?	Pardon?
Noch mal, bitte.	Once again, please.

12.1c How to ask for things to be said more slowly

(Etwas) langsamer, bitte!	(A bit) slower, please!
(Bitte) nicht so schnell!	Not so fast (please)!
Könntest du bitte etwas langsamer sprechen?	Could you please speak a bit more slowly?

12.1d How to find out the meaning of things and get the right word

Was heißt das?	What does that mean?
Was heißt „schlank"?	What does 'schlank' mean?
„Eine Taschenlampe"? Was ist das?	A '*Taschenlampe*'? What's that?
Was/wie heißt das auf deutsch/englisch?	What's that in German/English?
Wie sagt man...?	How do you say ...?
Ich habe das Wort vergessen.	I've forgotten the word

12.1e How to check information

Du heißt Peter, ja?	*You're called Peter*, aren't you?
Das ist blöd, nicht (wahr)?	*That's stupid*, isn't it?
Du hast „Ja" gesagt, oder?	*You said 'Yes'*, didn't you?
Stimmt das?	Is that right/correct/true?
Ist das richtig?	Is that correct?

12.1f   How to check and give spellings

Wie schreibt man das?	How do you spell that?
Schreibt man das mit *D* oder *T*?	Do you spell that with a *D* or a *T*?
Schmitt mit zwei T.	*Schmitt* with two Ts.

For more on the alphabet and spelling, see 11.1.

12.1g   How to say what you mean when you don't know the right word

Das ist so etwas *aus Metall*.	It's a sort of *metal* thing.
Ich brauche ein Dings [pl.: zwei Dinger].	I need a thingummy-jig.

Ich weiß nicht, wie man das sagt,
    aber *man schreibt damit*.
	I don't know how to say it
	    but *you write with it*.

12.1h   How to correct yourself

Verzeihung!/Entschuldigung!	Sorry!
Nein, nicht „*Heft*"–„*Hemd*" (meine ich).	No, not '*Heft*' – (I mean) '*Hemd*'.
Nein, ich wollte sagen...	No, I wanted/meant to say...

12.2   Dealing with people

See also 12.3 on plans and intentions.

12.2a   How to greet people

Guten Tag!	Hello. / Good day. / Good afternoon.
Grüß Gott!	Hello. (etc.) [in South Germany and Austria]
Guten Morgen!	Good morning!
Guten Abend!	Good evening!
Gute Nacht!	Good night!
Grüß dich, *Petra*!	Hi, *Petra*! [informal]
Hallo!	Hi!

12.2b   How to say goodbye

Auf Wiedersehen! / Auf Wiederschauen!	Goodbye! [slightly formal]
Auf Wiederhören!	Goodbye! [on telephone – formal]
Tschüs!/Tschüss!	Bye! [fairly informal]
Bis *morgen*!	See you *tomorrow*!

12.2c   How to wish people well

Alles Gute!	All the best!
Ich wünsche dir alles Gute!	I wish you all the best!
Herzlichen Glückwunsch!	Congratulations!
Gratuliere!	Congratulations!
Ich gratuliere (dir) (zu + *deinem Erfolg*)!	Congratulations (on your success)!
Herzlichen Glückwunsch zum Geburtstag!	Happy birthday!

Guten Appetit!	Enjoy your meal!
Mahlzeit!	Enjoy your meal!
Gute Besserung!	Get well soon!
Gute Reise! / Gute Fahrt!	Enjoy your journey! / Have a good trip!
Viel Spaß!	Have a good time!
Schlaf gut!	Sleep well!
Schönes Wochenende!	Have a nice weekend!
Schöne Ferien!	Have a nice holiday!
Frohe Weihnachten!	Merry Christmas!
Frohe Ostern!	Happy Easter!
Ein gutes neues Jahr!	Have a happy new year!
Prosit! / Prost! / Zum Wohl!	Cheers!
Prosit Neujahr!	Here's to the new year!

12.2d   How to reply to good wishes

Danke!	Thanks!
Danke, gleichfalls!	Thanks, the same to you!

12.2e   How to send good wishes to other people

Viele Grüße an *deinen Bruder*!	Best wishes / love to *your brother*!
(Einen) (schönen) Gruß an *Petra*!	Best wishes / my regards to *Petra*!
Grüß/Grüßen Sie *Peter* (von mir)!	Say hello to *Peter* for me./ Give my regards to *Peter*.

12.2f   How to ask for things

Ich möchte (bitte) (gern)...	I would like ... (please)
Kann ich bitte *ein Handtuch* haben?	May I have *a towel* please?
Kann ich bitte *auf mein Zimmer gehen*?	May I *go up to my room*?
Könnte ich bitte ...?	Please could I ...?
Ich habe/hätte eine Bitte.	There's something I'd like to ask for.

12.2g   How to ask for help

Hilfst du mir bitte?	Will you help me please?
Kannst du / könntest du ...?	Can you / could you ...?
Kannst du mir bitte helfen?	Can you help me, please?
Kannst du mir bitte *den Koffer tragen*?	Can you please *carry my suitcase* for me?
Kannst du mir bitte helfen, *den Sessel zu tragen*?	Can you please help me *to carry the armchair*?
Ich wäre sehr dankbar, wenn du mir helfen könntest.	I'd be very grateful if you could help me.
Hilfe!	Help!

12.2h   How to offer help

Kann ich dir helfen?	Can I help you?
Was kann ich für dich tun?	What can I do for you?
Kann ich (für dich) *abwaschen*?	Can I *wash up* (for you)?
Soll ich *die Tür aufmachen*?	Shall I *open the door*?

12.2i   How to thank people

Danke (sehr/schön).	Thank you (very much).
Vielen Dank (für alles).	Many thanks (for everything).
Vielen Dank / Danke für *deinen Brief*.	Thank you for *your letter*.
Danke, das ist/war sehr nett (von dir).	Thanks, that is/was very nice (of you).
Vielen Dank für deine Hilfe.	Thank you for your help.

12.2j   How to respond to thanks

Bitte (schön/sehr).	Don't mention it.
Gern geschehen.	It's a pleasure. [literally: 'gladly happened']
Nichts zu danken.	It was nothing. [literally: 'nothing to thank']

12.2k   How to enquire how people are

See also 10.30d.

Wie geht's (dir)?	How are things? / How are you?
Gut, danke (und dir?).	Fine, thanks (and you?).
Auch gut, danke.	I'm fine too, thanks.
Es geht mir { gut. / nicht so gut. / schlecht.	I'm { fine. / not very well. / not well.
Wie geht's *deinem Bruder*?	How's *your brother*?
Gut geschlafen?	Did you sleep well?
Schlaf gut! [**du** form]	Sleep well!

12.2l   How to apologise

(Oh) Verzeihung!/Entschuldigung!	(Oh) sorry!/pardon!
Entschuldige! [**du** form]	Sorry! / Excuse me!
Entschuldigen Sie!	Sorry! / Excuse me!
(Es) tut mir Leid.	I'm sorry (about that).
Es tut mir Leid, aber ... / dass ...	I'm sorry but .../that ...
Leider *konnte ich nicht kommen*.	Unfortunately *I couldn't come*.
Das habe ich nicht so gemeint.	I didn't mean it like that.
Das war ein Missverständnis.	It was a misunderstanding.

12.2m   How to make light of things

(Das) macht (doch) nichts!	It doesn't matter!
Das ist (doch) nicht (so) schlimm.	It isn't (such) a tragedy.
Schon gut!	It's OK.
Das kann passieren.	It can easily happen.
Vergessen wir das!	Let's forget (about) it!
Das ist nicht meine/deine Schuld.	It isn't my/your fault.

12.2n   How to agree

Das stimmt!	That's right/true!
Genau!/Eben!	Precisely!
Das glaube/meine ich auch.	That's what I think too.
Natürlich!	Of course!
Da hast du recht.	You're right there.
Einverstanden!	Agreed!

12.2o   How to disagree

Das stimmt nicht!	That isn't right/true!
Bestimmt nicht.	Definitely not.
Das glaube ich nicht.	I don't believe that.
Da hast du nicht recht.	You're wrong there.
Doch!	Yes! [contradicting someone's negative statement]

12.2p   How to complain

Was soll das?	What's going on? / What's that supposed to mean?
Das geht (doch) nicht!	That isn't on! / That's not possible!
Ich finde das nicht gut.	I think that's bad. / I don't agree with that.
Ich finde es nicht gut, dass …	I don't agree with the fact that …
So ein Mist!	How awful!
Das ist doch blöd/Blödsinn/Quatsch!	That's stupid/rubbish/nonsense!

12.2q   How to be unselfish

Bitte (schön/sehr)!	Here you are! / After you!
Nach dir/Ihnen!	After you!
Nimm du das doch!	You have it! / You take it!
Stört es, wenn ich *das Radio anmache*?	Will it bother/disturb you if I *turn the radio on*?

12.3   Plans and intentions

12.3a   How to make and ask for suggestions

Gehen wir *ins Kino*! [the 'let's' form – see 10.10.5]	Let's go *to the cinema*!
Wollen wir *ins Kino gehen*?	Shall we *go to the cinema*?
Kommst du mit?	Are you coming (with me/us)?
Kommst du mit *ins Theater*?	Are you coming (with me/us) *to the theatre*?
Spielst du Tennis mit mir? (present tense question)	*Will you play tennis with me*?

Hast/Hättest du Lust, *schwimmen zu gehen*?	Do you feel like *going swimming*?
Wie wär's [= wäre es] mit *einem Picknick*?	How about *a picnic*?
Wie wär's, wenn wir *ins Kino gehen*?	How about *going to the cinema*?
Ich möchte gern *fernsehen*.	I'd like *to watch TV*.
Ich möchte lieber *Musik hören*.	I'd rather *listen to music*.
Am liebsten möchte ich *Karten spielen*.	Most of all I'd like to *play cards*.
Was möchtest du machen?	What would you like to do?
Wir könnten in *die Disko gehen*.	We could *go to the disco*.
Ich habe eine Idee.	I have an idea.
Ich schlage vor, wir *bleiben zu Hause*.	I suggest we *stay at home*.
Was schlägst du vor?	What do you suggest?

12.3b   How to talk about plans and intentions

Ich gehe morgen einkaufen.	*I'm going shopping tomorrow.*
[present tense used with future meaning]	
Ich werde *morgen einkaufen gehen*.	I shall *go shopping tomorrow*.
[future tense – see 10.29]	

Ich	möchte* will* soll* muss*	*morgen einkaufen gehen.*	I	would like to want to am meant to have to / must	*go shopping tomorrow.*

[*see modal verbs – 10.8]

Was hast du *morgen* vor?	What have you got planned for *tomorrow*?
Ich habe vor *morgen einkaufen zu gehen*.	I'm planning to *go shopping tomorrow*.
Ich habe beschlossen *hier zu bleiben*. [see 10.32b]	I've decided to *stay here*.
Ich freue mich darauf.	I'm looking forward to it.
Ich freue mich auf *die Fete*.	I'm looking forward *to the party*.
Ich freue mich darauf *nach Bonn zu fahren*.	I'm looking forward to *going to Bonn*.
Hast du *heute Abend* Zeit/frei?	Are you free *this evening*?

12.3c   How to promise to do things

Ich *mache das*. [present tense]	I'll *do that*.
Ich *mache das* bestimmt / auf jeden Fall.	I'll definitely *do that*.
Natürlich *mache ich das*.	Of course *I'll do that*.
Kein Problem!	No problem!
Keine Angst (ich mache das)!	Don't worry (I'll do it).
Abgemacht!	Agreed! / That's settled!
Das verspreche ich (dir).	I promise (you).

12.3d How to find out (or check) what you should do

Was soll ich *machen*?	What shall I *do*? / What am I supposed *to do*?
Soll ich *den Tisch decken*?	Shall I *lay the table*?
(Bis) wann soll ich *zurücksein*?	When shall I *be back (by)*?
Wo soll ich *sitzen*?	Where shall I *sit*?
Ich *sitze hier,* ja?	I *sit here,* do I?
Darf/kann ich *hier sitzen*?	May/Can I *sit here*?
Muss ich *eine Karte kaufen*?	Must I / Do I have to *buy a ticket*?
Geht das (so)?	Is it all right (like this/that)?
Mache ich das richtig?	Am I doing it right?
Wir sehen fern, ja? Oder hast du etwas dagegen?	*We'll watch TV,* shall we? Or don't you like the idea?
Stört es, wenn *ich fernsehe*?	Will it disturb/bother you if *I watch TV*?

12.3e How to tell people what to do and what not to do

Komm doch mit!	*Come with me/us!*
Nehmen Sie doch Platz!	*Have a seat!*
Mach das nicht!	Don't do that!
Hör auf! / Lass das!	Stop it!
Das ist verboten.	That's not allowed.
Das darfst du nicht machen.	You musn't do that.

See also 10.10 on commands and 12.2g on how to ask for help.

12.3f How to arrange times and places

Wo/Wann treffen wir uns?	Where/When shall we meet?
Wo/Wann wollen wir uns treffen?	Where/When shall we meet?
Treffen wir uns *um acht.*	Let's meet *at eight.*
Treffen wir uns *um acht*?	Shall we meet *at eight*?
Treffen wir uns *vor dem Kino*?	Shall we meet *outside the cinema*?
Sagen wir, *Viertel vor acht vor dem Kino.*	Let's say *quarter to eight outside the cinema.*
Etwas später. / Etwas früher.	A bit later. / A bit earlier.
Geht das?	Is that all right?
Einverstanden?	Agreed?
Ist gut! / In Ordnung!	Fine!/OK!

12.3g How to handle invitations and treats

Ich möchte dich *zum Essen* einladen.	I'd like to invite you to *a meal.*
Hast/Hättest du Lust, *morgen zum Essen* zu kommen?	Do you fancy *coming for a meal tomorrow*?
Danke für die Einladung.	Thank you for the invitation.
Ich freue mich darauf.	I look forward to it.
Wann soll ich da sein?	When shall I be there?
Ich lade dich ein!	It's my treat! [= I'm paying for you]
Danke für deine Gastfreundschaft.	Thank you for your hospitality.

12.3h   How to hesitate about agreeing to something

Ich weiß nicht.	I don't know.
Das weiß ich noch nicht.	I don't know yet.
Ich weiß noch nicht, *was ich morgen mache.*	I don't know yet *what I'm doing tomorrow.*
Das kann ich noch nicht sagen.	I can't say yet.
Das muss ich mir überlegen.	I'll have to think about that.
Das/Es kommt darauf an.	It depends.

12.3i   How to refuse

Nein, das kann ich nicht.	No, I can't (do that).
Nein, danke!	No thanks!
Danke, das ist sehr nett, aber …	Thank you, it's kind of you, but …
Ich möchte gern, aber …	I'd like to, but …
Es tut mir Leid, aber …	I'm sorry, but …
Vielleicht *später.*	Perhaps *later.*

12.4   Explaining

REPORTING

12.4a   How to describe people and things

For more adjectives, see Chapter 2.

Er/Sie/Es ist *alt.*	He/She/It is *old.*
sehr *alt*	very *old*
ziemlich *alt*	quite *old*
Er ist/war *ein alter Mann.*	He is/was *an old man.*
Er hat/hatte *blaue Augen.*	He has/had *blue eyes.*
Es ist aus *Gold.*	It's made of *gold.*
Das ist/war ein Mantel mit *großen Knöpfen.*	It is/was a coat with *big buttons.*
Das ist/war der Mann, der … [relative clause – see 9.9]	That is/was the man who …

12.4b   How to say how to do things

Man *schreibt die Adresse oben rechts hin.*	You *write* / One *writes the address in the top right-hand corner.*
Du *machst es so.* [see 10.2–10.9 on the present tense]	You *do it like this.*
Dreh den Knopf nach rechts! [see 10.10 on commands]	*Turn the knob to the right!*

12.4c   How to say what happened

Use the perfect (**Perfekt**) or the simple past (**Präteritum**). See 10.12–10.27.

12.4d How to report what people said

Use reported speech. See 10.38.

12.4e How to say what you know or are sure of

Ich weiß, dass *die Bank heute geöffnet ist.*	I know that *the bank is open today.*
Ich weiß, *wo Peter wohnt.*	I know *where Peter lives.*
Ich bin sicher, dass ...	I am sure that ...
Petra fährt (ganz) bestimmt / sicher *mit.*	*Petra will* definitely *come with us.*
Petra fährt auf jeden Fall *mit.*	*Petra will* definitely *come with us.*
Sicher! / Bestimmt! / Auf jeden Fall!	Definitely! / Certainly!

12.4f How to say what you do *not* know for sure

Das weiß ich nicht genau. / Ich bin nicht ganz sicher.	I'm not quite sure.
Ich weiß nicht, *ob der Zug heute fährt.*	I don't know *whether the train runs today.*
Ich bin nicht sicher, ob ...	I'm not sure whether ...
Vielleicht *fahren wir morgen nach Ulm.*	Perhaps *we'll go to Ulm tomorrow.*
Eventuell *fahren wir morgen nach Ulm.*	Perhaps *we'll go to Ulm tomorrow.*
Wahrscheinlich *kann man hier Geld wechseln.*	*You can* probably *change money here.*
Es ist wohl *zu spät.*	*It's* probably *too late.*
Es sieht so aus.	That's the way it looks/seems.
Es scheint so.	That's the way it seems.
Es scheint, dass *Petra krank ist.*	It seems as if / that *Petra's ill.*
Das kann sein.	Maybe. / Perhaps.
Es kann sein, *dass sie krank ist.*	Maybe *she's ill.*

YOUR INCLINATIONS

12.4g How to say what you like or dislike

See also **10.30b** on **gefallen**.

<u>Activities</u>

Ich *spiele* gern *Tennis.*	I like *(playing) tennis.*

<u>People and general</u>

Ich habe *ihn/sie/es* gern.	I like *him/her/it.*
Ich mag *ihn/sie/es* (gern).	I like *him/her/it.*

<u>Foods</u>

Ich mag *Tomaten* (nicht gern).	I (don't) like *tomatoes.*
Ich esse (nicht) gern *Tomaten.*	I (don't) like (eating) *tomatoes.*

Things and places

Dieses Buch gefällt mir (gut).	I like *this book* (very much).
Diese Blumen gefallen mir (gut).	I like *these flowers* (very much).
Es gefällt mir *hier*.	I like it *here*.
Ich finde *das* sehr gut.	I like *that* very much.

12.4h   How to say what you prefer

See also 2.15 on how to compare.

Ich *spiele* lieber *Tennis* (als *Federball*).	I prefer (*playing*) *tennis* (to *badminton*).
Ich esse lieber *Äpfel* (als *Birnen*).	I prefer *apples* (to *pears*).
Ich mag/habe *Peter* lieber (als *Hans*).	I prefer *Peter* (to *Hans*).
Dieses Buch gefällt mir besser (als *das*).	I like *this book* better (than *that one*).
Ich finde *Paris* besser als *Rom*.	I prefer *Paris* to *Rome*.

12.4i   How to say what you like best

See also 2.16 on the superlative.

Am liebsten *spiele* ich *Fußball*.	I like (*playing*) *football* best.
Ich mag/habe *Peter* am liebsten.	I like *Peter* best.
Ich mag/esse *Tomaten* am liebsten.	I like *tomatoes* best.
Dieses *Buch* gefällt mir am besten.	I like *this book* best.
Ich finde *das* am besten.	I like *this/that* best.

12.4j   How to say what you wish for or dream of

Ich möchte (eines Tages) *Arzt / Ärztin werden*.	I'd like to *become a doctor* (one day).
Wenn es geht, möchte ich *nach Amerika fahren*.	If possible, I'd like to *go to America*.
Wenn ich *reich wäre*, würde ich … [see 10.39 on conditional sentences]	If I *were rich*, I would …

12.4k   How to give your opinions

Ich meine, dass *die „Cockroaches" eine sehr gute Band sind*.	I think that *the 'Cockroaches' are a very good band*.
Ich glaube, dass …	I think/believe that …
Ich finde, dass …	I think that …
Meiner Meinung nach *ist das dumm*.	In my opinion *that's stupid*.
Ich bin dafür.	I'm in favour (of it).
Ich bin dagegen.	I'm against (it).
Ich bin für + acc.	I'm in favour of …
Ich bin gegen + acc.	I'm against …
Was meinst du?	What do you think?

FEELINGS

12.4l   How to express pleasure and enthusiasm

Toll!/Prima!/Klasse! [informal]	Great!
Schön!	Great!/Nice!
Wie schön!	How nice!
Das ist aber schön!	That's really nice!
Das macht Spaß.	It's fun.
Das hat (mir) Spaß gemacht.	That was fun. / I enjoyed that.
Ich bin (sehr) glücklich.	I'm (very) happy.
Ich bin froh, dass *du da bist*.	I'm glad that *you're here*.
Es freut mich, dass ...	I'm glad that ...
Ich freue mich, dass ...	I'm glad that ...
Das freut mich!	I'm glad (about that)!

12.4m   How to express displeasure and horror

Ach, nein!	Oh no!
(Das ist) schrecklich!/furchtbar!	(That's) horrible!/awful!
Wie furchtbar!	How awful!
Ich habe einen Schreck bekommen.	I got a shock.
Ich bin/war (sehr) unglücklich/traurig.	I am/was (very) unhappy/sad.

12.4n   How to express anger

Ich bin/war (sehr) böse.	I am/was (very) angry/annoyed.
Ich bin böse mit *ihm*.	I'm angry with *him*.
Ich bin/war wütend.	I am/was furious.
Das geht (doch) nicht!	That isn't on!

12.4o   How to express astonishment

Ach!	Oh!
Ach so!	I see!
Nein!	No!
Na sowas!	Well I never!
Das ist/war eine Überraschung.	It is/was a surprise.
Komisch!	Funny!/Odd!
Komisch, dass *Petra nicht da war*.	It was odd that *Petra wasn't there*.

12.4p   How to express hopes

Hoffentlich *kommt der Bus bald*.	Hopefully *the bus will come soon*.
Ich hoffe, *der Bus kommt bald*.	I hope *the bus comes soon*.
Ich hoffe, dass *der Bus bald kommt*.	I hope that *the bus comes soon*.

12.4q   How to express fears

Hoffentlich *ist sie nicht krank*.	I hope *she isn't ill*.
Ich habe Angst.	I'm afraid.
Ich habe Angst, dass *sie krank ist*.	I'm afraid that *she might be ill*.
Ich habe Angst vor *dem Zahnarzt*.	I'm afraid of *the dentist*.

12.4r How to express disappointment

Schade!	Pity!/Shame!
Wie schade!	What a pity/shame!
Das ist aber schade.	That's a pity/shame.
(Es ist) schade, dass *Hans krank ist*.	It's a pity that *Hans is ill*.
Leider *mussten wir zu Hause bleiben*.	Unfortunately *we had to stay at home*.
Ich bin/war sehr enttäuscht (, dass ...)	I am/was very disappointed (that ...)

12.4s How to express relief

Zum Glück *hatte ich genug Geld*.	Luckily *I had enough money*.
Glücklicherweise *konnte ich zahlen*.	Fortunately *I was able to pay*.
Ich bin/war (sehr) erleichtert.	I am/was (very) relieved.
Endlich!	At last!
Wir sind endlich *angekommen*.	At last *we arrived*.
Endlich *sind wir angekommen*.	At last *we arrived*.

12.4t How to express indifference

Das ist mir (ganz) egal.	It's all the same to me.
Mir ist das (ganz) egal.	It's all the same to me.
Das interessiert mich nicht.	It doesn't interest me.
Meinetwegen.	It's OK as far as I'm concerned.

124u How to express boredom

Das ist/war langweilig.	It is/was boring.
Ich finde das langweilig.	I find it boring.
Das ist/war nicht interessant.	It is/was not interesting.
Ich langweile mich.	I'm (getting) bored.
[see 10.7 on reflexive verbs]	

12.4v How to express pain

See 10.30 on the dative used with verbs.

Au!	Ow!/Ouch!
Das tut weh.	It hurts.
Mein *Fuß* tut (mir) weh.	My *foot*'s hurting (me).
Ich habe *Magenschmerzen*.	I've got *stomach ache*.

13 How to write letters

13.1 Introduction

This skill is important in real life and in most examinations. In examinations, you have to write postcards and letters based on instructions from the examiners or as a reply to a postcard or letter printed on the examination paper.

Whatever letter-writing you have to do, you must first decide which of the three types is called for, and then stick consistently to the correct form. The three types correspond to the three words for *you*: **du**, **ihr** and **Sie** (see 4.3).

13.2 Letters to people you call *du*

These are usually letters to one friend of your own age, such as a pen-friend or exchange partner. You need the **du** form throughout – not **Sie**! Remember that the accusative of **du** is **dich**, the dative is **dir** and the word for *your* is **dein**. Traditionally these words were given a capital letter in letter-writing, but this is no longer compulsory.

This is the layout you must use. You do not write your full address at the top. Note all the details, including the use of capitals and punctuation:

Rainham, den 18. Oktober

Lieber Peter, / Liebe Petra,

danke für deinen Brief. Wie geht es dir?

Schreib bald!
Viele Grüße
dein/deine
Robert/Rebecca

Beginnings and endings

Typical phrases to use at the beginning of such letters include:

> danke für deinen Brief, den ich gestern bekommen habe.
> vielen Dank für deinen Brief.
> es hat mich sehr gefreut, deinen Brief zu bekommen.

Typical endings are:

> Lass bald von dir hören!
> Schreib bald (wieder)!
> Bis bald!

Closing greetings:

> Viele Grüße
> Herzliche Grüße
> Mit herzlichen Grüßen
> Alles Gute!

German-speakers like to send greetings to other people, like this:

> Viele Grüße, auch an *deinen Bruder und deine Eltern* [**an** + acc.]
> Schönen Gruß an *Petra*!
> Grüß bitte *Petra* von mir!

13.3 Letters to people you call *ihr*

These are mainly letters to more than one friend. The format and phraseology are very similar to the ones used for informal singular letters, except that you have to be very careful to use all **ihr** forms. The accusative and dative of **ihr** is **euch**, and the word for *your* is **euer**. Some of the letter phrases given in 13.2 need modifications:

> danke für **eueren** [OR: **euren**] Brief
> Lasst bald von **euch** hören! [see 10.10]
> Schreibt bald! [see 10.10]

Take particular care with the opening greeting. **Liebe Familie *Schmidt*** is no problem, but if two people are to be mentioned separately, the word **lieber/liebe** has to be repeated in the appropriate form, like this:

> Liebe *Karin*, lieber *Martin*,

At the end, remember to write **euer** (masculine) or **eure** (feminine) before your name, and *not* **dein** or **deine**.

13.4 Letters to people you call *Sie*

These are more formal letters written to people you would address as **Herr** or **Frau**. Often this means letters to hotels, tourist offices or other organisations, but it also might also include letters to the parents of a pen-friend. All the way through, you must use the **Sie** forms – not slipping back into **du** forms by mistake! The accusative of **Sie** is **Sie**, the dative is **Ihnen**, and the word for *your* is **Ihr**. These words always have a capital letter.

Beginnings and endings

The opening greetings are:

> Liebe Frau *Meyer,*
> Lieber Herr *Meyer,*
> Liebe Frau *Schmidt,* lieber Herr *Schmidt,* [when writing to a couple]

You use the above forms if you have already had friendly contact with the people. However, if you have to write to complete strangers, then you write:

> Sehr geehrte Damen und Herren,

If you are writing to a particular person whose name you know, put:

> Sehr geehrter Herr *Braun,*
> Sehr geehrte Frau *Braun,*

At the end of a formal letter, you put:

> Mit freundlichen Grüßen
> *Robert Davidson*

As in English formal letters, you may print your name below your signature to make sure it is absolutely clear.

13.5 Tenses to use in letters

All tenses can occur in letters, since you can write about the past, present and future. When you are writing about the past, both the perfect and simple past are equally correct (see 10.18).

13.6 Common structures to use in letters

Ich freue mich, dass ... [verb last]	I am glad that ...
Ich freue mich auf + acc.	I'm looking forward to [something].
Ich freue mich darauf ... zu + inf.	I'm looking forward to [doing something].
Ich habe vor ... zu + inf.	I plan/intend to ...
Ich habe beschlossen ... zu + inf.	I've decided to ...
Hoffentlich [verb second] ...	Hopefully ...
Ich hoffe ... zu + inf.	I hope to ...
Wie geht es + dat. ?	How is/are ... ? [see 10.30d]
Es geht + dat. (nicht) gut.	[Someone] is (not) well.
Wie gesagt, [normal word order]	As I said before, ...
Ich lege (dir/euch/Ihnen) + acc. bei	I'm enclosing ... (for you)
Es ist schade, dass ...	It's a shame/pity that ...
Es tut mir Leid, dass ...	I'm sorry (to hear) that ...
Entschuldige, dass ...	Forgive me for the fact that ...
Entschuldige, dass ich so schreibfaul bin.	Forgive me for being so lazy at letter-writing.
Es wäre schön, wenn ... [verb last in subjunctive II – see 10.39]	It would be nice if ...
Ich gratuliere (dir/euch/Ihnen) zu + dat.	Congratulations on ...

Ich wünsche dir/euch/Ihnen (alles Gute).	I wish you (all the best).
In meinem nächsten Brief [verb second] ...	In my next letter ...
Heute schreibe ich über + acc.	Today I'm writing about ...
Erzähle [**du** form] mir von + dat.	Tell me about ...
vom [date] bis zum [date]	from the [date] to the [date]

For more on dates, see 6.5.

13.7   Special structures for formal letters

Ich möchte + acc. für + acc. reservieren.	I'd like to book ... for ...
Hiermit bitte ich Sie ... zu + inf.	I hereby request you to ...
Ich wäre sehr dankbar, wenn ... [verb last in subjunctive II – see 10.39]	I would be very grateful if ...
Bitte teilen Sie mir mit, ob ... [verb last]	Please let me know whether ...
Ich habe die Absicht ... zu + inf.	I intend to ...

14 How to write past tense narratives

This skill is needed for some examinations.

14.1 The tools for the job

You need to know the following:

- the *simple past tense* (**Präteritum**: see 10.12–10.16), and especially the common strong and irregular verbs (marked with a bullet in the verb list in 10.43); verbs not on that list are regular and form the simple past tense with the **-te** endings (see 10.13);

- the *'verb second' rule* (see 9.4);

- how to link sentences using **und**, **aber**, **denn**, **sondern** and **oder** (which do not affect the word order at all – see 9.7);

- how to link sentences using subordinate clauses (see 9.8);

- how to use time expressions to begin sentences (see, for example, 7.9).

14.2 How to write your narrative

Here are some tips to help you.

Key sentences

A good method is to start by writing a list of key sentences – short, simple, past tense sentences, written one to a line, which tell the story in outline form. These can then act as a 'skeleton' for your story. This method stops you from getting into rambling, complicated sentences which are likely to go wrong. Also, key sentences are easy to check. You need to check for two things in particular: each sentence should contain:

- simple past
- the 'verb second' rule.

Here are some example sentences from a narrative about a holiday:

Ich **war** mit meinen Eltern auf Mallorca.
Wir **kamen** an.
Das Wetter **war** heiß.
Es **regnete** nur einmal.
Wir **verbrachten** zehn Tage dort.
Wir **wohnten** in einem guten Hotel.
Das Essen **war** ausgezeichnet.
Wir **lagen** am Strand.
Wir **schwammen** im Meer.

Wir **gingen** einkaufen.
Wir **kauften** Andenken.

Notice the simple past tense verbs, second in each sentence.

Time expressions

Add time expressions such as the ones in 7.9. These help link the story together. If you put a time expression at the beginning of any sentence, don't forget to rearrange the word order, so that the verb is still second. Based on the key sentences given above, you might write, for example:

Letztes Jahr war ich mit meinen Eltern auf Mallorca.
Jeden Tag lagen wir am Strand.

There is no need to begin every sentence with a time expression. Just a few will do.

Linking sentences together using *und*, etc.

Link some of the sentences using **und**, **aber**, **denn**, **sondern** and **oder**, which have no effect whatever on the word order (see 9.7):

Jeden Tag lagen wir am Strand **und** wir schwammen im Meer.

Here the second **wir** can be left out:

Jeden Tag lagen wir am Strand **und** schwammen im Meer.

Linking sentences together using subordinate clauses

Link some of the sentences together using subordinate clauses (see 9.8). These are desirable but not absolutely essential. Only do what you know is right! Here are two examples:

Als wir ankamen, war das Wetter heiß.
Wir schwammen im Meer, **weil das Wasser so warm war**.

Other refinements

Use other refinements if you feel able, such as **um ... zu** + infinitive (see 10.33) or reported speech (see 10.38).

Checking your final version

Write out a neat version of your finished narrative and then *check it carefully*! It is amazing how often people do not check their work and throw away marks carelessly.

14.3   Pitfalls to avoid

a   *Do not try to translate from English*. This is doomed to failure. Work from *German* vocabulary and expressions that you know.

b   Avoid getting into long complicated sentences. The word order and vocabulary are sure to go wrong.

c   Do not slip into the present tense in your story. This is a very common error indeed. The only place where the present tense may occur is in direct speech.

15 How to write German essays

This section is mainly for those who take German to a higher level.

15.1 Essay structure

The essay must have an introduction which considers the title and its implications. It may also indicate how you will tackle the subject.

There must then be a series of paragraphs, each of which makes one point. If possible, in each paragraph, you should state the point and then back it up with some kind of evidence or illustration. Many essays are of the **Vor- und Nachteile** type. First you state all the arguments in favour, then all the arguments against.

At the end, there must be a conclusion. This should not contain new arguments or facts, but should briefly summarise the essay. Often, this is the place to reveal a personal judgement.

15.2 Style

You must write in a formal style. This means that you avoid colloquialisms (**Umgangssprache**) such as **ein bisschen** and **kriegen**. Here are some alternatives:

For:	Use:
ein bisschen	ein wenig OR etwas
ein paar	einige
also [as a sentence opener]	darum
kriegen	bekommen
gucken	sehen
total [as an adverb]	ganz OR völlig

Formal style also means using *impersonal* expressions. You often need the word **man** (= *one*, see 4.2) This may seem stilted in English, but not in German:

Man sagt, dass Geld glücklich macht.
They say money makes you happy.

Wie kann man dieses Problem lösen?
How can you/one solve this problem?

15.3 Abbreviations

Do not use these in essays at all!

15.4 Clichés

There are many clichés which you can trot out in your essays. Some of these are handy and almost indispensable expressions such as **meiner Meinung nach**. Others help you to formulate sentences which have a definite German ring, e.g. **Den Ausschlag gibt, dass** ... (= *The deciding factor is that* ...). It is a good idea to build up your own list. Some are listed below. However, it is easy to overdo them, and they can easily distract you from concentrating on the 'meat' of your essay, which is far more important. So, use the clichés, but sparingly.

Introduction

Die Frage + gen. ist heißumstritten.	The question of ... is hotly disputed.
Diese Frage ist hochaktuell.	This question is extremely topical.
Diese Frage wird heute oft diskutiert.	This question is often discussed today.
Es gibt viele Gründe für + acc.	There are many reasons for ...
Es handelt sich hier um + acc.	We are here dealing with ...
Ich werde mich auf folgende Aspekte konzentrieren:	I shall concentrate on the following aspects:

General

... spielt eine große Rolle.	... is very relevant.
... spielt keine Rolle.	... is irrelevant.
Alle sind sich einig, dass ...	Everybody is agreed that ...
Einerseits ... [verb second]	On the one hand ...
Andererseits ... [verb second]	On the other hand ...
Aus diesem Grund ... [verb second]	For this reason ...
Daher/Deswegen/Deshalb/Darum ... [verb second]	That is why ...
Darüber hinaus ... [verb second]	Over and above that ...
Das hängt mit + dat. zusammen.	This is connected with ...
Es ist kein Wunder, dass ...	It is no wonder that ...
Es steht fest, dass ...	It is indisputable that ...
Hier stellt sich die Frage, (ob) ...	Here we must ask (whether) ...
Ich bin der Meinung, dass ...	I am of the opinion that ...
im Gegensatz zu + dat.	in contrast to ...
im Vergleich zu + dat.	in comparison with ...
In diesem Zusammenhang ... [verb second]	In this connection/context ...
In mancher Hinsicht ... [verb second]	In some respects ...
In vielen Fällen ... [verb second]	In many cases ...
Kurz: [normal word order]	In short:
Meiner Ansicht nach ... [verb second]	In my view ...
Meiner Meinung nach ... [verb second]	In my opinion...
Nach Meinung der Experten ... [verb second]	In the opinion of experts ...
Umfragen haben gezeigt, dass ...	Surveys/Polls have shown that ...

Interpreting data

Zwanzig Prozent der Befragten sagten, dass ...	Twenty per cent of those questioned said that ...
Die Zahlen/Statistiken beweisen, dass ...	The figures/statistics show/ prove that ...
Diese Grafik zeigt deutlich, dass ...	This graphic clearly shows that ...
Eine große/knappe Mehrheit ist für/gegen + acc.	A big/bare majority is/are in favour of / against ...
Rund ein Viertel [sing.] ist der Meinung, dass ...	Around a quarter are of the opinion that ...
Über die Hälfte [sing.] meinte, dass ...	Over half gave the opinion that ...

Conclusion

Aus all dem muss man schließen, dass ...	From all this, one has to conclude that ...
Leider ist keine Lösung in Sicht.	Unfortunately, no solution is in sight.
Man kann nur hoffen, dass ...	One can only hope that ...
Nach Abwägung der Argumente komme ich zu dem Schluss, dass ...	After weighing up the arguments, I come to the conclusion that ...
Wir sehen also, dass ...	So we see that ...
Die aufgeführten Argumente beweisen, dass ...	The arguments made here show that ...
Alles in allem ... [verb second]	All in all ...
Zusammenfassend möchte ich betonen, dass ...	In summary, I would like to emphasise that ...

15.5 *Therefore/so*

The basic word to use is **darum**. This also covers *so* and *and so* in the meaning of *therefore*. Do not use **so** or **und so** in this meaning. When you want to express a strong logical link (i.e. your new sentence is a logical deduction from the previous one), you can use **daher**, **deswegen** or **deshalb**.

15.6 *Finally...*

English essays often feature *Finally* ... somewhere near the end — either to introduce the last point in the argument, or else to introduce the conclusion. There is no obvious German equivalent. **schließlich** and **zum Schluss** both mean *in the end* or *after all*, so they are not appropriate. Some possible solutions are given in 15.4 above. However, the best way is generally to omit any translation of *finally*. You can often make your point just as well without it.

15.7 English words with more than one German equivalent

There are many of these, and choosing the right word is sometimes tricky. The following notes should be of some help. (For verbs with more than one German equivalent, see 10.42.)

bad

- not up to the expected standard **schlecht**
- absolutely bad **schlimm**

careful

- cautious(ly) **vorsichtig**
- meticulous(ly) **sorgfältig**

Note also the verb *auf*passen (auf + acc.):

Pass auf!
Be careful!

Pass auf die Autos **auf!**
Be careful of the cars.

Du solltest besser **aufpassen.**
You ought to be more careful.

difficult

- onerous, arduous, hard **schwer**
- complicated **schwierig**

different

- not the same item; changed (from) **ander-** [**anders** when standing alone] **als**
- not like each other; various **verschieden**
- varied **unterschiedlich** [partly overlaps with **verschieden**]

Examples:

Peter ist **anders als** sein Bruder.
Peter is different from his brother.

Udo und Jan sind **anders.**
Udo and Jan are different (from others).

Udo und Jan sind jetzt **anders.**
Udo and Jan are different now [= changed].

Udo und Jan sind **verschieden.**
Udo and Jan are different [= not alike].

Sie haben **verschiedene** Ideen.
They have different [= various] ideas.

Sie haben **unterschiedliche** Ideen.
They have different [= varied] ideas.

even

The basic word is **sogar**. This can be used in the majority of cases where English has the word *even*. Before nouns, **selbst** and **auch** are very frequent alternatives.

> **Auch/Selbst/Sogar** die Engländer können fleißig sein.
> Even the English can be hard-working.

- *not even* must be **nicht einmal** (colloquially: **nicht mal**).
- *or even* is **oder gar**.

 eben does not mean *even*. It means *just* (e.g. **Der Zug ist eben angekommen**).

most, mostly

- *mostly* is **meistens**.
- *most* is **der/die/das meiste**, usually it is in the plural, which is **die meisten**.
- *most people* is **die meisten Leute**.

number

- mathematical number; amount   **die Zahl (-en)**
- amount   **die Anzahl (-en)**
- one of a sequence or list   **die Nummer (-n)**
- figure (i.e. as written/printed)   **die Ziffer (-n)**

Examples:

> Die **Zahlen** beweisen, dass ...
> The figures demonstrate that ...

> Die **Zahl/Anzahl** der Menschen, die Drogen nehmen, nimmt ständig zu.
> The number of people taking drugs is constantly rising.

> Ich wohne **Nummer** elf.
> I live at number 11.

> Zweihundert in **Ziffern**: 200.
> Two hundred in figures: 200.

people

- **Leute** (which only rarely appears without a marker or adjective before it) refers to people as a group, as a mass.

- **Menschen** (plural of **der Mensch**) refers to people as individual human beings:

> Viele **Leute** haben Vorurteile.
> Many people have prejudices.

> Viele **Menschen** wurden verletzt.
> Many people were injured.

Remember that **man** is sometimes the appropriate word (see 4.2).

they

Often in English we use *they* to refer to vague, unspecified people (e.g. *They say yogurt is good for you*). In German, **sie** can only be used to refer back to a specific, recently mentioned, plural noun. Otherwise use **man.** (See 4.2.)

work

• work, employment, labour	**die Arbeit**
• profession (i.e. a learned skill)	**der Beruf (-e)**
• career (over time)	**die Karriere (-n), die Laufbahn (-en)**
• appointment, post	**die Stelle (-n), die Stellung (-en)**
• job (especially temporary)	**der Job (-s)**
• job, workplace	**der Arbeitsplatz (¨e)**

Note the following:

Ich gehe **zur** Arbeit.
I go to work.

Ich bin **bei der** Arbeit.
I am at work.

Ich **bin berufstätig**.
I have a job. [a skilled/professional one]

Diskriminierung **am** Arbeitsplatz
discrimination in the workplace

neue Arbeitsplätze schaffen
to create new jobs

Index